Bright Id
World of Work

Written by Jane Fulford, Merryn Hutchings
and Alistair Ross

Contents

Published by Scholastic Publications Ltd,
Marlborough House, Holly Walk,
Leamington Spa, Warwickshire CV32 4LS.

© 1989 Scholastic Publications Ltd

Written by Jane Fulford, Merryn Hutchings
and Alistair Ross
Edited by Christine Lee
Sub-edited by Jane Morgan
Illustrations by Ann Johns, Maggie Mundy
Agency

Printed in Great Britain by
Loxley Brothers Ltd, Sheffield

ISBN 0 590 76016 5

Front and back cover: designed by Sue Limb,
Photographs by Martyn Chillmaid.

Introduction

WHY LOOK AT THE WORLD OF WORK?

Work is a vital ingredient of our society – indeed, of nearly every society. We depend, for almost all the material goods and services we need, on someone else being able to provide them better than we can do ourselves, in return for the work that we can do. We often define ourselves by our work. If there's no work for us, we are unhappy. Such a vital ingredient of society ought to be important to children too – and this importance should be reflected in their curriculum.

Perhaps even more importantly, studying the world of work gives opportunities for children to learn about economic concepts, how things may be in short supply or how they are priced; social concepts, how workplaces are organised, and who is in charge; and lastly scientific and technological concepts, how machines are used, automation and control.

Industry is not a straightforward term. In the context of this book, it doesn't mean simply manufacturing industry. Indeed, only a few of the examples in this book concern making things. There is extraction, distribution, transport, retailing, services such as teaching and refuse collection; all are industrial tasks.

In the context of the primary school, industries must be local. Nearly every school is situated near some form of industry, and the essence of the direct experience and active learning that this book takes as a central theme is that the children must visit the workplace as often, and for as long, as possible. Local visits, repeated over three or four weeks, are much more useful than coach journeys to distant locations.

5

WHAT TO DO

Visit a workplace near the school where the children can follow the stages of production, interview workers and management about their jobs, or shadow a worker for half a day.

Back in the classroom children can:

- Talk about their experiences and reflect on them through role-play, art, model-making or creative writing.
- Carry out some part of the processes they saw in the workplace.
- Investigate scientific or technological ideas they encountered in the workplace.
- Find out about the history of the workplace or product.
- Explore the organisation of the workplace.

Children generally come back from a workplace visit filled with enthusiasm and interest, and produce their own ideas about the direction they want the project to take.

Invite people to visit the school to talk about their work. These may be staff from a workplace you have visited, or parents, governors or friends who have skills or experience which will be useful in a class project. Question sessions are generally more worthwhile than giving talks, as the children's questions help the visitors pitch their information at the right level for the class. Children are often more confident asking questions in the classroom than on a visit.

Organise a simulation of a workplace in the classroom. Ask the children to take on roles of workers, management, customers, suppliers, and so on, then act out a problem or situation. This helps them to understand how other people may feel about their work, and how conflicts may arise and be solved.

Set up a mini-enterprise whereby the children form an organisation which provides a service or makes a product. They have to find out what people want, decide what resources they need, organise themselves, advertise and market their service or product, and decide what to do with the profit (if any). The children do all the planning and make all the decisions; this is a good way to get children to work co-operatively, and to involve them in all the processes of a workplace.

SAFETY ASPECTS

Before a visit to a workplace check whether there are any dangers for the children such as unguarded machinery, steep steps, dust or fumes. Check the insurance position with your LEA and with the workplace.

HOW TO MAKE CONTACT

Small workplaces are often more satisfactory than larger ones. Children can relate better to small numbers of adults and build up a clearer picture of the whole organisation. If you want to study a large firm, divide the class into groups and let each group look at different sections of the organisation. Avoid the packages that some large firms provide. Try to persuade them to adapt to fit in with your needs.

It is best to choose a workplace close to the school, preferably within walking distance. This allows for the possibility of several visits and more informal contacts. The children may already be familiar with a local workplace and know some of the people who work there. Some of the employees may be parents at the school.

The best way to make arrangements with a workplace is through a personal contact – a parent, friend or colleague. School governors and support staff are often good sources of information. If you wish to visit a larger firm, and have no personal contact, write a brief letter to the personnel manager explaining why you want to study this workplace and what it would involve. If you choose a smaller firm, approach the manager. Follow up your letter with a phone call or visit the firm yourself. Leave plenty of time to make the arrangements. If you have trouble finding a suitable workplace, you may have to change your plans.

A preliminary visit to the workplace by the teacher is essential. You will need to be very clear about your objectives. Firms will not respond favourably to vague ideas. Be prepared to show what areas of the curriculum you could include in the project and what you hope the children will gain from the contact. Links with industry should be a two-way process. Think how the project might benefit the firm: better community relations, ideas for

advertisements, and market research on a product or service are all possibilities. So too is the valuable experience for younger employees of explaining their jobs or showing children round the workplace.

Remember that many adults have little experience of young children and little understanding of the way a primary school works. You will need to explain the capabilities of your class.

Before the visit, finalise all the practical details, such as the constraints of timing, health and safety aspects, toilet facilities, the name of your contact at the firm, and precise numbers of children and staff for the visit.

Your first attempts to make contact with a workplace may get a negative response. Some firms will refuse without explanation, or on health and safety grounds, or because a visit from a class of children will disrupt schedules and involve the firm in financial loss. If you still think that a visit to this firm would be valuable, explain how your class would benefit from this contact. You may have to look elsewhere – but don't be discouraged.

THE ORGANISATION OF THIS BOOK

This book is divided into sections, which concentrate on ideas that can be developed around a particular sector of industry and are based on visits, on simulations and on mini-enterprises.

If there's a particular industry near you that you would like to use, try the contents page to see if there's a suitable idea here. But remember, there may be ideas about other workplaces that you could easily adapt to fit your needs. Try looking firstly at other ideas in the same sector of work, and move out from there.

WORK AND NON-WORK

Defining 'work' is not as simple as it may seem, and this section offers a number of ideas for children to explore. Is work always paid? What about work in the home? How does this differ from the teacher asking a child if he has finished his work? What about people who do things for a living that we do for recreation, such as the professional footballer?

PEOPLE GETTING RAW MATERIALS

This covers extracting raw materials from the ground, farming and fishing. Because this varies throughout the country, it's certain that some areas won't apply to your school. But a surprising number will: start making enquiries. The point of this section is to help children to see where familiar products come from. Some of the ideas may seem a bit far-fetched, but they can all be done with primary-aged children. Six schools did visit an on-shore oil rig – so think big!

PEOPLE BUILDING THINGS

The construction industry involves building homes, shops, roads and factories. This section focuses on what children can see and do in the world of building. Much active learning on a large site may be impossible, but visits to small sites, and meeting people off-site, are much easier. Building involves close co-operation between people with a range of different skills, all working together in a complex way – but the very tangible and understandable results make this an excellent area for primary-aged children to study.

PEOPLE MAKING THINGS

Manufacturing is no longer the backbone of British industry, but it's still a vital and large component. One of the key variables as far as primary schools are concerned is the size of the workplace. If it is too large an

enterprise, or if there are too many workers involved, it becomes hard for young children to keep hold of the overall pattern – and too easy to lose sight of the individuals. Try to aim for a workplace that employs the same number or fewer than the number of children in the school.

PEOPLE MOVING THINGS

The transport industry is a major employer, and it's a relatively easy one for children to understand. Many primary schools are within easy reach of railway stations and bus garages; some can get to canals, airports and seaports. Looking at these sorts of industries can easily lead to a study of transport links across the country and even the world – but it's usually better to start with a thorough exploration of your local depot or network.

PEOPLE SELLING THINGS

Napoleon once described England as a nation of shopkeepers, and the retail industry offers children many opportunities for exploration. Almost every school in the country must be within walking distance of a shop or two. Get children to look at large and small shops. Ask them to think about where the money goes. Many infant classes already simulate shops in the classroom: this section offers suggestions for taking this a few steps further.

PEOPLE ENTERTAINING PEOPLE

Some people's work is helping other people relax. This section is full of ideas for how children can examine aspects of the leisure industry.

PEOPLE HELPING PEOPLE

Service industries are everywhere, and are easy for children to understand; the hospital, the school and the emergency services are familiar to many children. But have they considered how they are provided and organised? How many people in a hospital are nurses and doctors, and how many provide the essential back-up services of catering, cleaning, laundering, portering and keeping the accounts and payroll going?

MAKING WORK EASIER

The final section offers some ideas for looking at how jobs can be made simpler and more efficient. There are scientific and technological ideas to explore and simulations to try.

Merryn Hutchings and Alistair Ross work at the Primary Schools and Industry Centre, The Polytechnic of North London. Jane Fulford was a seconded teacher-fellow at the centre. The centre organises short INSET courses for primary teachers, and publishes teachers' materials, resource lists and case studies.

Details are available from: the Primary Schools and Industry Centre, The Polytechnic of North London, Prince of Wales Road, London NW5 3LB; tel: 01 - 607 2789.

Work and non-work

Choosing a job

Age range
Seven to eleven.

Group size
Whole class.

What you need
The class for discussion.

What to do
Ask the children to imagine that they are looking for their first jobs. What things do they think will be important to them? Their answers will probably include some of the following:

- good pay;
- a sympathetic and considerate boss;
- being in regular work with no risk of being made redundant;
- long holidays;
- a chance to learn a skill;
- good working conditions (what do they think are good working conditions?);
- being able to work independently and use their own ideas;
- doing a job they think they would enjoy (what would that be?);
- a job where they can get promotion;
- a chance to be useful to others (how could they do this?);
- easy work (what do they think would be easy?);
- a job where they will have responsibility.

What else do the children think will be important to them when they look for their first jobs? Discuss what jobs the children think they would actually like to do,

and why. How much do they know about the jobs they are suggesting?

Follow-up
Invite some young people who have recently started work to visit the classroom and talk with the children about their jobs and how they chose them.

11

Job application

Age range
Seven to eleven.

Group size
Whole class working in small groups.

What you need
Job advertisement pages from local and national newspapers, application forms for a range of jobs, pens, paper.

What to do
Ask each group of children to investigate a different type of job, using the advertisements to find out what qualifications and personal qualities are required. Then ask them to investigate the application forms to discover the categories of information required.

Discuss with the whole class what jobs need doing in the classroom: paint pot monitor, gardener (responsible for watering classroom plants) and so on. If the whole class is involved in a mini-enterprise (see 'Pizzas, biscuits or buns?' on page 78) these could be real jobs in the enterprise.

Ask each group to design an advertisement and a job application form for a different classroom job. For a sample job application form see photocopiable page 123. Invite the children to fill in application forms, and ask each group to hold interviews for the job they advertised. Successful candidates will hold their jobs for a limited period, decided in advance (perhaps a month).

Follow-up
Invite the local Employment Officer, the careers teacher from the local secondary school, or someone from the Job Centre to talk with the children about qualifications required for different jobs, and the procedures involved in getting a job.

Pay packet

Age range
Seven to eleven.

Group size
Whole class working in pairs.

What you need
Newspapers advertising jobs and indicating pay scales, or figures stating how much people are paid in different occupations; pencils, paper.

What to do
Give the class a list of different jobs. It is important that they have some idea of the nature of each job or the sort of qualifications needed. One suggestion for such a list would be:
- cleaner;
- police constable;
- fire-fighter;
- waitress/waiter;
- factory manager;
- doctor;
- dancer;
- housewife/husband;
- factory worker;
- Prime Minister;
- lorry driver;
- teacher;
- typist;
- ticket collector;
- nurse;
- childminder.

Tell the children to imagine that they are in charge of how much people earn. Each pair decides which of

these jobs ought to receive most pay. Write 16 next to that job, 15 by the one that should be paid next most, and so on. The job that the children think should be paid least will have 1 next to it.

Discuss the results with the class. How did they decide which jobs should be paid most? Children tend to be more influenced by the idea of working hard and long hours than by ideas about responsibility. They also question the common assumption in our society that brain work is worth more than physical work.

Follow-up
Get the children to look at all the information that you have collected about rates of pay for various jobs. Can they work out the rank order of what each of the jobs on their list is actually paid? Are they surprised by what they find? Do they think that the value given to different jobs is correct?

13

On the dole

Age range
Nine upwards.

Group size
Groups or whole class.

What you need
One, or preferably several, unemployed people. Try asking at a local centre for the unemployed. Clearly it is important to have people who are willing to discuss with the children issues involved.

What to do
Ask each unemployed person to discuss with a group of children:
- how they came to be unemployed (for example, redundancy or school leaver who has not had a job);
- whether they have applied for jobs, and if so, what has happened;
- how they spend their time now they are unemployed;
- the problems of unemployment (for example, lack of money and lack of occupation).

Follow-up
Invite a local Employment Officer or similar to discuss unemployment with the children.
- Why are so many people unemployed?
- Is anyone to blame?
- Could everyone get jobs if they moved to other areas of the country or acquired different qualifications?
- Is unemployment caused by developments in technology?
- Is it necessary for the economy to have people who are unemployed?

Child labour

Age range
Seven to eleven.

Group size
Whole class.

What you need
Paper, graph paper, pencils, felt-tipped pens.

What to do
Get the class to write about any work they do. It is up to them to decide what is and what is not work.

They will probably mention some of the following:
- helping with chores (may be paid, or unpaid work);
- school work;
- homework set by school;
- practising a musical instrument.

A few children may also have experience of employment; for example, acting or appearing on a commercial.

Make a large graph showing the work experience of the class in different categories.

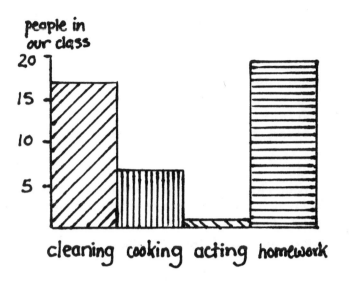

Discuss how the children decided what is and what is not work by looking at the following points:
- Does work have to be paid?
- Is work doing something that you have to do, and don't want to?
- Is work something which is physical rather than mental?
- Is work 'not fun'?

Adults describe work in all these different ways; the point of the exercise is to help children realise that there is no single narrow definition of work.

Follow-up
Investigate the laws concerning employment of children. When were these made? Are they still appropriate? Do the class feel that they should have more opportunities for working to earn money?

School work

Age range
Nine upwards.

Group size
Small groups, pairs.

What you need
Tape recorders, clipboards, paper, pencils.

What to do
Ask the groups to discuss which activities at school are work, and which are not. Discuss also how they distinguish between the two. Is it a clear-cut distinction, or is there a range of different types of work? Are the same subjects always work, or are there occasions when they become 'not work'?

As a class, discuss ideas about school work, then ask the children in pairs to interview a child from another class and discover if they think the same.

Follow-up
Many children think that maths is real work, and that subjects like art, music and PE are not work.

Do the same things apply when they think about adult jobs? Do they think a bank clerk works harder than a dancer or musician? Discuss this with the class.

Housework and DIY

Age range
Five to nine.

Group size
Large group or whole class.

What you need
Two co-operative friends who are prepared to talk to the class about the work done in their homes and to explain who does it. It would be helpful if the people invited had different arrangements in their homes; for example, one family where the mother goes out to work and the father does the housework, and one vice versa. This would help challenge sex-role stereotypes.

What to do
Get the children to tell you what work they think is done in a home. Some children may think that work only means working to earn money; if this question arises you will need to discuss it.

For each job the children suggest, ask your friends to tell the children who does it in their home. Children may also like to contribute and say who does each job in their houses. Their contributions should be welcomed, but no-one should be made to feel that they have to contribute if they don't want to. Some children feel embarrassed because they have an au pair, or they do not have a dishwasher. The purpose of the activity is to help the children to understand that different households arrange their work in different ways, and that all arrangements are equally acceptable.

Follow-up
Make model houses, and model people to put in them doing different jobs. The children can decide whether they want to have, for example, father washing-up and granny doing the decorating.

Growing your own

Age range
Five to nine.

Group size
Class organised in groups.

What you need
A local allotment holder or gardener who grows fruit and vegetables to eat.

What to do
Arrange a visit to a garden or allotment where fruit and vegetables are grown. Ask the gardener to show the children what is being grown, and to talk with them about the work involved, and the reasons for growing fruit and vegetables, such as:
● they taste better when fresh;
● it saves money;
● gardening is enjoyable;
● gardening is a healthy occupation.
  Ask the gardener if he thinks gardening is work. Does it make him tired? Does he get any pay or reward?
  Back in the classroom discuss how people decide what is work and what is not.

Follow-up
Grow something to eat in the classroom, playground or school garden. This could be mustard and cress, lettuces or other vegetables. Salad crops are probably best because you get quick results.
  When your produce is ready, find out how much it would cost in a shop. Then calculate how much you have spent on seeds, fertiliser etc. The difference between the two prices, if any, will represent the labour costs, the transport costs, the middle man's profit and the shopkeeper's profit. The children's labour, of course, is free, as was the vegetable gardener's. On the other hand you have probably had to pay more for your seeds and fertiliser because you are not buying in bulk.
  Eat or sell your produce.

Charity fund-raiser

Age range
Seven to eleven.

Group size
Whole class, working in groups.

What you need
Information about a variety of charities. A voluntary worker involved in fund-raising (preferably from the charity the class selects for their efforts), pencils, paper.

What to do
Divide the class into groups and distribute all the information you have collected about the needs of various charities. Ask each group to read them, discuss their relative merits, and decide which one they would most like to support. Then ask each group in turn to present their chosen charity and their reasons for wanting to support it.

After a general discussion, decide which charity or charities the class will support.

Next ask the class to think of a variety of ideas for raising money. Invite a person involved in raising money for charity to visit the class to discuss these ideas.

Remember that often it is the children's own parents who end up producing most of the money. Can the class involve a wider public?

Having decided how to raise money, help the children organise every stage of whatever they have decided to do – advertising, collecting a float of change from the bank, or whatever may be appropriate for their ideas. (See 'Start up capital' on page 81 and 'Hidden persuaders' on page 82.)

Involvement in all stages of the fund-raising process is an enterprise from which children can learn a variety of skills and concepts: discussion, negotiation, capital, price, value, and so on. Schools are frequently involved in efforts for charity, but this can also become a valuable part of the children's education if they are more closely involved in the whole process.

Follow-up
Arrange for the children to make a visit to their chosen charity or to have a visitor to tell them more about the way their money is being spent.

The class could also investigate the whole rationale of the charity. Why is this particular need met from voluntary giving rather than by the government?

Women's work, men's work

Age range
Seven to eleven.

Group size
Large groups or whole class.

What you need
A number of relevant testimonies from men and women acquired from visits to various workplaces, photographs from magazines of people at work, the results of surveys made by children.

What to do
Start a discussion on whether certain jobs should only be done by men or by women. Occupations that you might like to introduce into the discussion are nursery teachers, airline pilots, cooks, nurses, refuse collectors, among many others.

Do the children recognise constraints? Do they see some sexual division of labour when they look around them? Why is it there? Do they agree? What evidence have they?

Questions such as these often lead to a lively debate.

Follow-up
Ask the children to put their points of view to workers and managers at a workplace.

Voluntary work

Age range
Nine upwards.

Group size
Whole class, possibly organised in groups.

What you need
A voluntary worker (other than a fund-raiser). It could be, for example, someone who runs a book trolley in a hospital, or who reads to a blind person, or who gardens for somebody old. Many local authorities have an organiser who co-ordinates voluntary work and may be able to put you in touch with someone.

What to do
Charities often involve children in fund-raising, but less commonly in voluntary work. This gives children a one-sided view that charity is all about raising money.

Invite the voluntary worker to come to talk to the children about their work, and the reasons why they do it. Why is this work done on a voluntary basis instead of being paid work? Why does this worker choose to do voluntary work instead of (or as well as) having a job?

Arrange for the children to become involved in some kind of voluntary work. This should be a one-off piece of work which does not require long-term commitment which the children might not be in a position to give.

People getting raw materials

Gone fishing

Age range
Seven to eleven.

Group size
Small groups or the whole class.

What you need
Access to a fishing port, clipboards, pencils, tape recorders, cameras, polythene bags.

What to do
Arrange to visit a fish market when sales are in progress. This may be earlier than usual school hours.

Watch how the fish are landed and auctioned. Tape record the auctioneer's patter (see if the class can decipher what it means later). When the sales are over, there may be a chance to talk to port and auction officials about their work. Use the polythene bags for collecting wholesalers' labels that are stuck on the crates of fish as they are bought.

Follow-up
In the classroom, work out the way that the fish are sold and distributed across the country. Ask the children why they think wholesalers and retailers are necessary. Invite a local fishmonger to talk to the children.

Make a display of the fish wholesalers' labels.

Make up a song based on the auctioneer's patter.

Coal mine

Age range
Seven to eleven.

Group size
Whole class.

What you need
A visit from a coal miner, perhaps with some underground equipment, tape recorders.

What to do
Interview a miner about his work underground, and about the support services on the surface. Coal mining is an activity that depends on complete co-operation, interdependence and confidence in all the other miners. A preparatory discussion with the class might help them understand this.

Encourage the children to explore the reasons why coal miners depend so much on each other.

Follow-up
It might be possible to visit the surface working of a coal mine. It will not be possible to go underground (but in some mining areas there are simulations that children will be able to visit).

Investigate the history of coal mining.

Clay pit

Age range
Nine upwards.

Group size
Whole class for visit, breaking down into four or five groups.

What you need
An open-cast clay pit that your class can visit, camera, tape recorders, clipboards, paper, pencils.

What to do
Arrange a visit to an open-cast pit so that the children are able to talk to workers in various departments. Preferably, the class should first tour the whole works, so that they can get an idea of the entire enterprise.

Organise the visit so that each group talks to people working in different departments. Get the children to make notes, tape record conversations and take photographs if this is possible as they look around.

Back in the classroom exchange information and build up an idea of how all the departments depend on each other.

Find out if the clay has to be processed at the site before it is sent to customers. Find out who the principal customers are. How does the clay reach them? Has it always taken this route?

Follow-up
Back at school, try to work out how the workplace is organised. Ask each child to draw one or two workers, then cut out the drawings and assemble them as a hierarchy chart. Alternatively, arrange the drawings as a hierarchical mobile.

Ask the children to make models of the workers that they met (in clay, of course!).

Fish farms

Age range
Seven to eleven.

Group size
Variable.

What you need
A commercial fish farm that the class can visit, clipboards, paper, pencils, cameras, books on fish care, fish tank, goldfish, fish food.

What to do
Visit the fish farm and talk to the workers about how the job is done, and how the fish are marketed.

Find out about the difficulties of keeping fish. Then try to overcome these by keeping some fish in school.

Organise a mini-enterprise based on breeding goldfish for sale at a school fête. This may also involve the production of books on fish care, and the sale of fish food.

Follow-up
Invite someone from the fish farm to see the mini-enterprise in operation, and to advise on the organisation that the children have developed.

Milking time

Age range
Five to eleven.

Group size
Whole class, divided into large groups where necessary.

What you need
A dairy farm where your class can see milking in progress. Normally, milking time is either very early in the morning, or late afternoon, which makes visits in school time difficult. However, a few farms will arrange to milk during school hours so that school parties can visit. Your LEA science or industry adviser should be able to help. Alternatively, some zoos arrange milking sessions.

A milk bottling plant could be the focus of either a second visit or an alternative to the dairy farm.

On both visits you will need clipboards, paper, pencils, cameras and tape recorders.

At school, after the visit you will need full fat milk and soured milk, rennet, live yoghurt, cream, sugar, soft fruit, a jar with a lid, a bowl, muslin, a vacuum flask and refrigerator.

What to do

Visit a dairy farm at milking time. Find out about how much milk each cow can produce. How long does it take to milk the cow? Is the milk processed on the farm? Where does it go to?

At the bottling plant watch the milk bottling process. Ask the workers where they get their milk from. How is it processed?

In school, try making various products from milk.

- Butter: shake full fat milk in a jar for over half an hour (pass it around the class).
- Cottage cheese: place soured milk in a bowl, with rennet. Strain in muslin until it forms a solid lump.
- Yoghurt: add a little live yoghurt to milk warmed to about blood heat. Keep it this temperature for a day (well insulated, or in a wide-necked vacuum flask).
- Ice-cream: place a mixture of cream and milk, with some sugar and crushed strawberries (or other soft fruit) in the ice-compartment of a refrigerator. Stir the mixture at intervals as it freezes.

Follow-up

Make a chart showing the journey of the milk from cow to shop, and another showing all the various products which use milk.

Have you any wool?

Age range
Five to nine.

Group size
Small groups.

What you need
A visit to a sheep farm. Samples of sheep's wool, detergent, water, dyeing pan, bleach or dyestuffs (such as onion skins, blackberries or synthetic dyes), two metal combs, spindle or pencils, Plasticine and knitting yarn, knitting needles or weaving loom.

What to do
If your class can visit a sheep farm, ask the farmer how sheep are fleeced, and which are the best sorts of sheep for this.

Collect some sheep's wool. Encourage the class to process it into knitting yarn.

This will involve:
- Cleaning the wool: remove the obvious dirt, then wash the wool thoroughly in detergent and rinse it clean.
- Bleaching or dyeing the wool: try household bleach (carefully!), or boil the wool with natural dyestuffs (onion skins make a fine yellow), or use synthetic dyes (which may not need heating).
- Carding the wool: use two metal combs, with the wool on a flat surface, to pull the fibres so that they run in the same direction.
- Spinning the fibres into a strand: this is traditionally done with a spinning wheel or a drop spindle (not as easy as it looks!). Alternatively, push a pencil through a lump of Plasticine and carve a notch in the pencil. Attach a piece of knitting yarn to the pencil as in figure 1, then separate the fibres at the end of the piece of yarn. Twist some of the fibres from the sheep's wool to merge with the yarn. Twist the weight to make it rotate and let it slowly fall as more fibres are added. The weight gives a slight twist to the emerging yarn. This isn't easy either!

Ask the children to knit or weave their yarn into a small square.

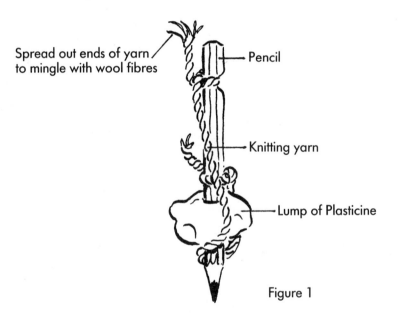

Spread out ends of yarn to mingle with wool fibres — Pencil — Knitting yarn — Lump of Plasticine

Figure 1

Follow-up
Contact commercial producers of wool. Ask how they prepare yarn from fleeces.

On the farm

Age range
Five to eleven.

Group size
Whole class for visit, small groups for classwork.

What you need
Access to a farm that grows crops, polythene bags for collecting soil samples, jars with lids, scales, seeds, flower pots, pencils, paper.

What to do
Visit the farm and get the children to ask the farmer about the crops, and how decisions are made about what to sow. Ask about the types of soil that are found on the farm and collect samples. Augment these with other samples from the school grounds and the children's own gardens.

In school, divide the class into groups and ask them to examine soil types by mixing samples of soil with water and observing the layers that form: small stones at the bottom, then grit and sand, fine sand, and then clay. Fresh humus material may float. How do the soils differ?

Use more samples of the soil to test water-retaining powers and permeability. Will water run straight through it? Will it collect on the surface and not get through? Use accurate scales to find out how quickly water evaporates from different types of soil.

Grow seeds in different soils. Allow them all equal access to sunlight, warmth and water. How do the plants vary? What could cause this?

Quarry

Age range
Seven to eleven.

Group size
Whole class for visit, small groups for class work.

What you need
Access to a working quarry. Clipboards, paper, pencils, camera, tape recorders, small polythene bags, labels, model-making materials.

What to do
Visit the quarry and talk with the managers and workers about their work.

Look at the machinery being used. Can the children work out the functions of each machine?

Collect rock samples. If the rock contains fossils, ask if you can look for them in the quarry.

In school, organise an exhibition based on the visit. This could contain a section about how the quarry works, perhaps with a model of the quarry, photographs and even a tape recording — and a section on the fossils and rock samples that the children have collected.

Oil rig

Age range
Nine upwards.

Group size
Whole class for visit, small groups for follow-up.

What you need
Check with major oil companies or your local authority if any on-shore drilling is taking place in your area. If so, ask if your class may visit. They will need old clothes and boots; the oil company will probably supply helmets.

Back in the classroom the children could look at the products of oil; the conservation factors in getting the oil out; or how oil is formed.

Follow-up
Design and make a balsa-wood rig. Visit a local petrol station to see how the end products are sold.

What to do
Visit the rig. The children should be able to talk to workers for some of the time, see machinery, and look at drill samples.

Making paper

Age range
Seven to eleven.

Group size
Two to four.

What you need
A visit to a paper manufacturer, old newspapers, a tray for water, wallpaper paste, a rectangular wooden frame with fine muslin fixed tautly over it.

What to do
Arrange a class visit to a paper manufacturer and talk to the workers about the paper-making process.

In the classroom, ask the children to make their own paper. Get them to tear newspaper into small pieces, then mix this thoroughly with water and wallpaper paste. Leave this papier mâché mixture to soak overnight.

The next day, place the wooden frame in a tray of water, then add some of the papier mâché and let it spread out in the water. When the papier mâché has formed a thin layer across the muslin, slowly lift the frame. Allow the sheet of papier mâché to dry, then carefully remove it from the frame.

Follow-up
Experiment with the colours of the papier mâché. Can the sheets be bound together in a book?

Baking bread

Age range
Five to nine.

Group size
Class or large group visits; variable size group work in the class.

What you need
A visit to a wheat-growing farm, ears of wheat, sharp knife, two large flat stones, a culinary sieve, yeast, salt, water, a stove.

What to do
Visit a farm with the class to see wheat being harvested. Talk with the farmer about where the wheat is sent. Collect ears of wheat to take back to school.

In school carefully cut open a grain of wheat and show the children the flour inside.

Get the children to break up the ears of wheat, to roll the grains in their hands to remove the outer husks, and then grind them between the two stones. (Using a coffee grinder can speed things up!) Sieve the resulting mix of husk and flour.

Make bread with the flour the children have ground.

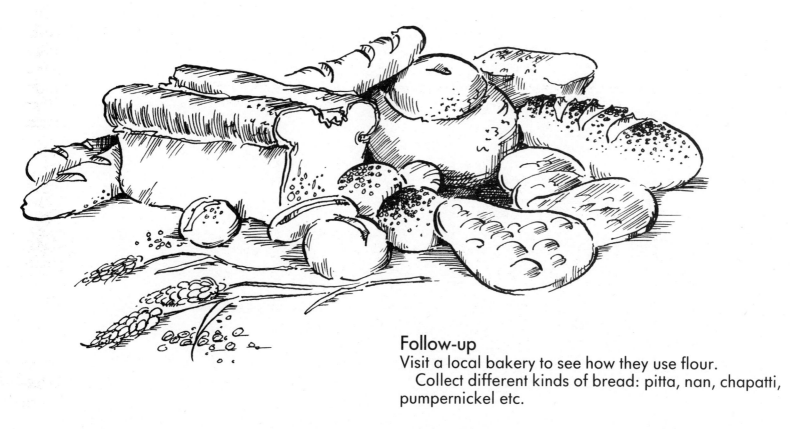

Follow-up
Visit a local bakery to see how they use flour.

Collect different kinds of bread: pitta, nan, chapatti, pumpernickel etc.

People building things

A woman's place?

Age range
Nine upwards.

Group size
Groups of about five children.

What you need
Classroom space.

What to do
This is a role-play exercise which raises the questions: what happens when a man applies for a job on a building site? What happens when a woman applies for a similar job?

Cast the children in each group into roles. One can play a building site manager wanting workers to fill several jobs on the site; two can be workers already on the site. The fourth child, a boy, then comes along looking for work. Do not tell the fifth child, a girl, what her role will be yet.

Let the manager interview the boy looking for work, and probably take him on.

Then brief the girl. Tell her (not the others) that she has all the qualifications for the job; she's trained for it, is strong, and has had previous experience. Then she applies for the job.

What is the manager's reaction? Does he ask her qualifications? (Did he ask the boy's?) Does he accept her qualifications, or does he look for more excuses?

Try the exercise out with several groups at the same time, so that they can't compare results until afterwards. Then discuss how people react in situations like this.

Follow-up
This role-play might be more useful if, after you have tried it, the children speak to someone from industry or a trade union about job qualifications and/or equal opportunities.

Write to the Equal Opportunities Commission for information on discrimination at work. The address is: Equal Opportunities Commission, Publicity Department, Overseas House, Quay Street, Manchester M3 3HN. Collect pictures of women performing 'traditional' male roles.

Discuss other jobs that are usually done only by members of one sex (nursery nurses, priests . . .).

Team-work

Age range
Five to eleven.

Group size
Variable, starting with individuals and getting larger.

What you need
Lego bricks or similar construction materials.

What to do
This activity centres on the discussions that take place during the construction of models. Often children discover that working together brings problems – of sharing, of frustration, of communication. The object of the exercise is to help talk about these difficulties.

Make up simple identical models for each member of the class. Put all the other pieces away.

Ask each child to look carefully at the model, and then to take it completely to pieces. Ask them to time how long it takes to re-assemble the model. They should write this down, and then try again. Do they get faster? Why? Why are some people faster than others?

Then form pairs. Each pair must co-operate to build two models. Afterwards, ask them how they did this. Was it easy working together? Repeat the operation. How do they feel?

Then group the pairs into fours, and carry out the same procedure again. Then form eights. How do they work together? Is it faster? Is it easy to organise? Is it easy to share skills and to work with people with different ideas?

Building together

Age range
Five to eleven.

Group size
Groups of seven or eight, or whole class.

What you need
A convenient building site (preferably a large one) that can either be visited or clearly observed from a viewing platform; clipboards, paper, pencils.

What to do
Ask the children to observe all the different jobs being done. If they aren't able to talk to the workers, ask them to work out (with your help if necessary) what they think is going on.

They could list what each individual does, a different child observing each worker. They could draw some of the operations.

Back in school, discuss all the different jobs. There may have been surveyors, clerks, lorry drivers, machine operators, crane drivers, bricklayers, carpenters, plasterers, decorators, glaziers, roofers, plumbers and electricians. Why are there so many different jobs? Why can't one person do all of them?

Introduce the idea of specialised jobs that allow some people to concentrate on and train for particular tasks. Do they think that this means that the standard of work is better, or that the job is completed more quickly, or both? Does it involve special training?

Follow-up
Make a collage of all the tasks that have been seen, showing the whole site in operation.

In order

Age range
Nine upwards.

Group size
Large group or whole class.

What you need
A building site (as in 'Building together' see page 37) where the clerk of works or site manager is able to talk with the class; clipboards, paper, pencils and/or tape recorders.

What to do
Talk to the clerk or manager about how the work is organised on the site. Who has to start work on the site? For how long? Who can follow next?

Is this order of workers essential? What happens if one group doesn't get their bit right? Who has to put it right? Whose work is upset?
Can some groups work side by side?

Follow-up
Ask the class to make a diagram showing the sequence of jobs on the site. Mark how long each task takes. How fast could the building be completed? Can anyone work independently of the others? The discussion in this exercise centres around inter-dependence.

Skilled work

Age range
Five to eleven.

Group size
Groups of up to ten children (for the visit).

What you need
A local builder, perhaps specialising in repair work, or the local council's direct works depot; clipboards, paper, pencils, perhaps a camera and tape recorder.

What to do
Small builders are different from large construction firms; the workers are more likely to have a range of specialist skills, and to be involved in repairing or restoration work.

Arrange to take a group of children to visit either the builder's yard or a site on which they are working. Get the children to note all the different jobs each person can do and to ask about the skills that are required. How do the workers function together as a team? How do they decide how a job is to be tackled?

Compare the organisation of this work to that on a larger construction site (see 'Teamwork' on page 36 and 'Building together' on page 37).

Follow-up
Some schools have involved children in planning and carrying out small-scale building projects in the school grounds. If you do this, don't forget to ask the builders to visit, to comment on progress and offer advice.

Designer playground

Age range
Five to eleven.

Group size
Initially groups of around three; these may combine in later stages.

What you need
A playground, paper, pencils, catalogues from builders' merchants and school playground suppliers . . . and perhaps much more!

What to do
Ask each group to think of ways in which the playground could be improved. For example, does it need murals, more equipment, a re-organisation of space or new lines for games?

When the groups have drawn up their plans, give them the catalogues, and ask them to work out what will be needed to put each plan in operation. You may need to combine two or three groups for this.

Can older children work out the cost of the plans?

Follow-up
If you and your headteacher like the plans, ask the children to try to raise the cash to implement them.

Building skills

Age range
Seven to eleven.

Group size
Variable, up to whole class size.

What you need
An amenable craftsperson in the building trade, tape recorder, perhaps a camera, paper, pencils, crayons.

What to do
Invite your craftsperson to school to talk with the class about what he does, and how he acquired his skills. He may want to bring in some items or tools to show the class, or to demonstrate some activity.

Ask the children to find out more about the training and work involved. Perhaps groups could agree beforehand to specialise in asking questions about particular areas.

After the visit ask the class to create a display of pictures and writing that bring together all the information that they have collected.

Roof first?

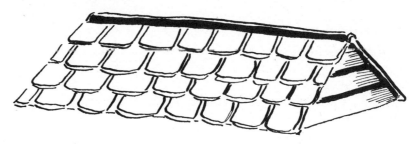

Age range
Seven to eleven.

Group size
Several small groups co-operating to construct a class model.

What you need
Card, adhesive, paint, brushes, scissors, other modelling materials and tools.

What to do
Assemble a class model that shows all the stages of a building being constructed. The class will probably need to do some fieldwork before they start.

In what order do the stages have to be tackled? One logical idea might be to build the roof first, so that if it rained while the rest of the house was being built the workers would keep dry!

One group could prepare the base of the model, with all the service pipes and wires. Another might make foundations to fit over this; another tackle the structural walls, another the interiors, another the timber for the roofing skeleton, and another the tiles.

Groups will need to co-operate closely to make sure that the parts fit together correctly.

Beginnings

Age range
Seven to eleven.

Group size
Small groups.

What you need
Photograph or drawing of an old building that has had parts of it developed and updated, paper, pencils.

What to do
Look at the photograph or drawing of an old building and try to work out how the building was originally constructed. What must have been built first? Make a series of drawings to show the various stages. Incorporate both the building of the original structure and the addition of later parts (and perhaps the demolition of other parts).

Alternatively, groups could start the other way round, by taking away what they think is the most recent addition, and moving backwards through time.

Follow-up
A series of books by David Macaulay – *Cathedral*, *City* and *Pyramid* (all published by Collins) – shows this process with line drawings that children can pore over for hours.

Will it last?

Age range
Seven to eleven.

Group size
Small groups working together.

What you need
Range of building materials, including wood, breeze-block, plasterboard, nails, paper, pencils.

What to do
Buildings are usually built to last. Ask the children to devise tests for each of these materials to see what might destroy them. If they succeed in making any of the materials deteriorate, the next task will be to find some kind of treatment that will make them last longer.

For example, the children might readily get the wood to start rotting by leaving it out in the open and damp. Can they then treat a similar piece of wood (for example, with coats of oil-based paint) to protect it from the same endurance test?

Try letting water freeze over the breeze-block, or letting rain fall on the plasterboard and nails. Each material may need a different type of finish in order to preserve it.

43

Reinforced concrete

Age range
Seven to eleven.

Group size
Small groups.

What you need
Sand, gravel, cement, water, scales, an old bucket,
some short steel rods, a large plastic tray, two bricks.

What to do
Concrete may be very strong, but will varying the
proportions of the ingredients change the strength of the
product? Will adding reinforcement help?

Get the children to devise tests for this. Use the scales
to weigh proportions as accurately as possible, before
mixing the concrete in an old bucket.

One suggestion might be to cast pieces of concrete in
a tray. This will give uniform-sized pieces of the test
material. Put some steel rods into one of the mixtures to
see if that makes any difference to its strength. It will
take three days or so to dry out properly, but can be
removed from the tray much sooner.

Ask the children to think of various ways to test the
strength. Resting the block on the bricks, and inviting
increasingly more children (of known weight) to stand
on it could be fun.

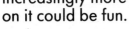

Brick-up

Age range
Five to eleven.

Group size
Small groups working co-operatively.

What you need
Wooden bricks, building bricks, cement, sand, a trowel.

What to do
Simply experiment with building walls. Ideally, these should be for a real purpose, such as building raised flowerbeds, but this may not always be possible. The class might experiment with different arrangements (using wooden bricks) before starting on the real thing.

Follow-up
Ask a professional bricklayer to look at and comment on the children's work.

People making things

Production flow

Age range
Nine upwards.

Group size
The whole class, breaking down into large groups.

What you need
A light engineering factory that the class can visit, preferably not too large. Clipboards, paper, pencils, cameras, tape recorders.

What to do
Take the class through the production processes – starting from the incoming stores, through all the workshops, to finishing, packing and the outgoing stores. Ask the workers in each section to explain what happens in their department. Visit the offices and the designers.

Get groups to write about different departments. Then ask how they are related. At what stage are the goods when they are transferred between each department? Construct a flow diagram to show how partly finished goods move. Do departments depend on each other? How?

Follow-up
Act out the work at the factory, a small group of children representing each department. What happens when the flow of goods is upset?

Discuss how workers in each department have different skills. Why is this? Is it an advantage for everyone to have specialised work?

47

Working together

Age range
Seven to eleven.

Group size
The whole class divided into small groups.

What you need
A local small printer, cameras, tape recorders, clipboards, pencils, paper.

What to do
Make two visits to a printer. Before the first, do very little except ask the children what they think they might find. Who will work there? What sort of jobs will they do?

During the visit, encourage the children to ask questions, make notes and drawings. Back in school, run through their previous ideas. Did the visit meet their expectations? (It probably did not – and realising this will help them see that preconceptions can be misleading.)

Talk about the different tasks at the printers – getting orders, typesetting, proof-reading, making plates, machine-minding, and so on. It may all be computerised. Is one job more important? What would happen if anyone didn't do their work properly?

On the second visit, encourage more structured questions. Who helps whom? Who sends on work to the next person? Try to develop the concept of interdependence through interviews and discussion.

Follow-up
See 'Read all about it!' on page 54 for activities on newspapers.

Pollution

Age range
Nine upwards.

Group size
Small groups, using the whole class.

What you need
This will vary according to the nature of the pollution: plastic bottles for water samples, white cloth, pegs, white tiles and petroleum jelly for air samples, tape recorders for noise, camera.

What to do
Choose a local workplace and see if you can find out how its waste products affect the locality. Does it produce smoke? (You could use a camera to record this.) Is there air pollution? (Use damp white cotton strips hanging in the air, and compare these with a control; or smear a white tile with petroleum jelly to pick up dirt in the air.) Where does solid waste go? What about noise?

Follow-up
Compare the results with those of a non-industrial site, or a different industry.

Prepare a report on pollution. Speak to the factory manager about the children's findings. What could he or she do?

What do people living and working in the neighbourhood think?

Smoothing the flow

Age range
Seven to eleven.

Group size
Small groups.

What you need
Squared paper, felt-tipped pens.

What to do
Most workplaces are adapted according to the building in which they are situated. As the enterprise grows, so the space is adapted or extended.

After a visit to a manufacturer, ask the children to identify the main stages or processes that went on. What would be the logical way to organise these? How is it different from the actual design of the factory?

Ask groups to prepare alternative layouts for the factory to make production easier. This could be adapted into a flow-chart.

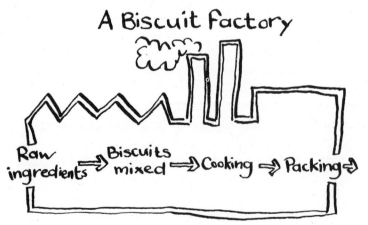

Can the children identify the places where things may get held up? How can bottle-necks be avoided?

Follow-up
Ask the groups to make models of how their new design would look.

Show the designs and models to the workers and managers of the factory that was visited. Ask them for their comments.

Musical machines

Age range
Five to nine.

Group size
Whole class or groups.

What you need
Scrap materials from a visit to a factory, such as off-cuts of metal, plastic, pipes and tubes, nuts and bolts; metal file, hacksaw, yoghurt pots.

What to do
Design and make musical instruments from scrap materials, making sure that any sharp edges are filed down.

Make chimes from metal off-cuts and bars. Cut them into varying sizes with a hacksaw to achieve different notes.

File the inside and outside edges of tubes and pipes to remove any sharp surfaces, then produce musical notes by blowing across the end.

Use the nuts and bolts in empty yoghurt pots to make shakers.

Experiment with other items to make percussion instruments.

Ask the children to compose a piece of music using their instruments to describe a day in the factory.

Follow-up
Use scrap to make a collage of the factory. Or use scrap parts as stencils when painting.

Production line

Age range
Five to seven.

Group size
Groups of up to twelve children.

What you need
Lego or some similar construction materials; a very long strip of paper, sticky tape or stapler.

What to do
In this activity the children explore different ways of organising the making of a simple model from a construction kit.

Show the class how to assemble a particular model. Then get them to make several models on their own. Can they think how they might make them in less time?

Fit the strip of paper around the top of a row of tables, so that if forms a continuous length across and under the surface and fasten the two ends together. Position the children along the strip, each with a particular sub-assembly task to do.

Then, using 'teacher power', start the strip moving as a conveyor belt, with each child adding their parts to the assembly as it moves past.

Try moving the paper very slowly, or very quickly, and then talk about the children's reaction to this.

Which process was most enjoyable to the children? Which made the most models? How else could they organise the work?

Where did it come from?

Group size
Small groups.

What you need
A range of items of scrap material – perhaps from one of the many industrial scrap projects for schools.

What to do
Show the children a range of scrap materials and ask them what they think was being made when these materials were used. There are often many clues – the type of material, the shapes that have been cut out, and

so on. Ask the class what machinery must have been used to cut or form the materials.

Can the class think how the scrap materials might be used (other than in classroom modelling and collage)?

Follow-up
Draw machines that might produce something with the scrap items.

53

Read all about it!

Age range
Five to nine.

Group size
Whole class, arranged in groups as necessary.

What you need
Paper, pencils, access to some kind of duplicator such as a stencil or photocopier, a typewriter or a word processor.

What to do
Produce a class magazine or newspaper. It might have one or several issues, but the important thing is to encourage the children to plan the enterprise themselves.

They will need to consider:

- how to reproduce it;
- how much it will cost;
- what jobs are required;
- whether they have the necessary skills between them;
- who will decide who does what;
- how they will finance the project;
- who will want to buy and read the paper;
- what sort of news will interest the readers;
- how they will decide what to include;
- how they will distribute and sell the paper;
- what to do with any profits that they make.

There are no 'correct' answers to any of these questions. The essential point is that any class of children can come to some kind of decision for themselves on each of these points, and that as they progress their decisions should become more informed – and better!

Safety at work

Age range
Seven to eleven.

Group size
Large groups.

What you need
A visit to a factory, paper, pencils, felt-tipped pens, paints, brushes.

What to do
All workplaces are safe if the rules are followed. Ask the children to look particularly at the potential points of danger in any manufacturing enterprise that they visit.

Where might things go wrong? What are the rules about safety? Are they followed? Who makes sure that they are followed?

Don't forget the health questions: does anything happen that might cause damage or harm in the long term?

What happens if an accident does occur?

Get the children to ask the workforce for their opinions, as well as the managers responsible for health and safety. The local trade union representative might offer particularly valuable insights.

Get the class to prepare a safety campaign for the workplace. Make leaflets and posters promoting safety at work.

Follow-up
Are the safety rules in your school adequate? With an experienced safety-investigation team, now's the chance to overhaul the school's procedures!

Who says what?

Age range
Seven to eleven.

Group size
Divide the class into four groups.

What you need
Space for drama work.

What to do
Ask each group to take on the role of a group of people working in a factory. Give the four groups the following briefs:

- Workers on the production line: two of them have been dared to borrow some expensive materials to show their friends in the evening. A production line supervisor sees them.
- Trade union shop stewards: their task is to look after their members' interests, to make sure that the workers aren't unreasonably sacked, and that their jobs are safe.
- Production line supervisors: they are responsible for keeping production going. One of them notices two workers pocketing some materials. There are strict rules that this must not be done.
- Production managers: they are responsible for keeping the factory going, and ensuring that it makes as much money as possible. They have made strict rules about theft from the company.

Let the workers and supervisors talk first, out of earshot of the other two groups. Then get the workers to talk with the shop stewards, and the supervisors with the managers.

What happens next? Do the managers summon the workers? Do the workers ask for shop stewards to come with them? Do the shop stewards ask to see the managers? What action is taken?

Follow-up
After the role-play, get the children to explain their actions to each other.

Apprenticeship

Age range
Five to eleven.

Group size
Various.

What you need
The chance to watch a craftsperson at work, access to materials similar to those that she uses.

What to do
Take the class to visit a craftsperson and to watch her at work.

Encourage the children to make something similar, using the same sort of techniques, processes and materials. Even quite young children can attempt relatively sophisticated items.

Discuss with the class the difficulties they had. How easy is it to learn the necessary skills?

Follow-up
Invite the craftsperson to see the class at work and to discuss their tasks with them.

People moving things

Tickets please

Age range
Five to seven.

Group size
The whole class.

What you need
A local railway station, spare classroom furniture, paper and pens for making tickets, toy money.

What to do
Arrange to visit a station and, if possible, take a ride on a train.

If the station is local, one of the children's parents may work there. Invite a station worker to visit the school to talk to the children: a train driver or ticket collector, for example.

Turn a corner of the classroom into a station waiting-room or a station buffet. Make imitation train tickets, then set up a ticket office by the door and ask visitors to the classroom to buy a ticket using toy money.

Follow-up
Make a large collage of a train with several coaches. The children can draw their own faces and place them in the coaches looking out of the windows. Make books about the station and the jobs that people do there.

Travellers' fare

Age range
Nine upwards.

Group size
The whole class.

What you need
A local railway station, clipboards, pencils, paper.
Contact British Rail Education Department for materials
and information. The address to write to is British Rail
Education Service, Room 118 (CP12), Euston House,
24 Eversholt Street, London NW1 1DZ.

What to do
Organise a visit to a local station. Before the visit,
discuss the public facilities that are needed at a station.

At the station carry out a survey of the facilities and
amenities. Is there a waiting room suitable for mothers
with babies? Are there toilets available and if so, are
they clean? Is the buffet open at times when travellers
need food? Is there a left luggage facility?

In the classroom, draw up a report on your findings.

Follow-up
Look at the problems for passengers who are disabled.
Choose a disability to consider in greater depth. What
are the facilities like for people who are blind or in a
wheelchair? What suggestions can the children make to
improve these facilities?

If appropriate, take the children's suggestions to the
station-master.

Bus garage

Age range
Seven to eleven.

Group size
The whole class or group of about eight.

What you need
A local bus garage that will welcome a visit, pencils, paper.

What to do
Prepare for the visit by practising interviewing techniques. What sort of questions might the children want to ask? Encourage the use of direct questions that ask why, how and what. Practise interviewing someone in school about their work, perhaps the headteacher or one of the support staff.

Ask the children to make a list of the jobs that they expect to see being done at the bus garage. Can they think of any jobs that have to be done which they might not see such as cleaning, delivering supplies to snack bars etc. Visit the garage and talk to some of the people about their jobs. Make a note of all the different jobs that are being done. Were there any surprises?

Follow-up
Draw up a questionnaire for a passenger survey. Include questions about distance, destination, frequency of use and the facilities used. For a sample questionnaire see photocopiable page 124. Return to the garage and carry out the survey. In the classroom draw a graph showing where the passengers were travelling from and to. Mark the routes on a large scale map. Put together the material from the survey and extract information about passenger use and satisfaction. Consider presenting the results to the bus garage.

Canal

Age range
Five to eleven.

Group size
The whole class or group of about eight.

What you need
A local canal, and contact with someone who lives and/or works on the water. Contact the British Waterways Board for information and resource materials. The address to write to is the British Waterways Board, Melbury House, Melbury Terrace, London NW1 6JX. Pens, pencils, paper and clipboards.

What to do
Take the children for a walk along a canal bank. Ask them to make a note of the people and the boats they see: barges, pleasure boats, people fishing and walking dogs, conservation and repair workers. Are any people working? If so, what are they doing? Discuss the difference between 'work' and 'leisure'. Look for signs of changing times along the canal: marks from horse ropes, disused warehouses, old water-wheels, new uses for old buildings etc. In the classroom, make a chart of the people seen on or along the canal. If possible, take the same walk at the weekend. Note the differences.

Follow-up
Invite a canal worker to talk to the children about their work. Collect a range of books about canal life and compare the work you saw being done with the work that was done in the past. Compare living on a boat with living in a house or a flat. What are the advantages or disadvantages of living on water? Make a chart showing the similarities and differences between life on the water and life on land. Try some traditional canal art, such as castles and flowers painted in bright colours. Make some papier mâché plates and decorate them with paints and ribbons.

Wheels

Age range
Seven to eleven.

Group size
The whole class.

What you need
An old bicycle, pencils, paper, bicycle spanner, thin card, pair of compasses, needle, thread, scissors, a bicycle repair shop that would welcome a visit.

What to do
Ask the children to make a close observational drawing of the bicycle. If possible, let them take the bike apart and draw some of the parts separately. Look at the shape of the frame and see how it supports the rider. Look at the wheel. Why is the tyre full of air? What would it be like with a solid tyre? Count the spokes on the wheel.

Draw two large circles on thin card to represent wheels. Mark the number of spokes round the wheels at regular intervals. Link the spokes with the hub of the wheel with a needle and thread. Cut out different-sized wheels. Compare the number of turns needed to travel a certain distance. Which requires most effort, a large wheel or a small one?

Visit the bicycle shop. Talk to the shopkeeper about the different types of bikes, new developments, plastic bikes, racers, mountain bikes etc. Ask the shopkeeper about repairs and maintenance of bikes, dangerous aspects and so on.

Follow-up
Arrange a visit from the local council's road safety officer to talk specifically about bicycle safety on the roads. If possible, ask the children to bring their bikes to school for safety checks. Design and make posters on bicycle maintenance and safety to display around the school. Look at the development of the bike, and design a bike for the twenty-first century. It could be a fantasy bike.

Travelling light

Age range
Seven to eleven.

Group size
The whole class.

What you need
A large cardboard box, brown wrapping paper, sticky tape, string, scissors, arrangements with a local station or road haulage firm, information from the Post Office about parcel post.

What to do
Arrange a contact as far away from the school as possible. Decide upon a reason for sending a parcel; it may be full of letters to children in another school, for example.

Discuss with the class how best to send large parcels and packets. Wrap up a large box. How can you make it really secure?

Arrange to visit the railway station, road haulage firm or post office depot to send the parcel. Find out which route the parcel will take, whether by road or rail. Gather as much information as possible about the journey of your parcel. How many people will handle it? How long should it take? Will it change trains or vans? How will it reach its final destination?

Follow-up
At school, trace the route on a large map. Ask your contact to telephone you as soon as the parcel arrives. If your contact is another school, make a pen-friend arrangement and continue the project by looking at the Post Office and the delivery of letters.

Post office

Age range
Five to nine.

Group size
Class or group of any size.

What you need
Information materials
from the Post Office,
cardboard,
scissors,
adhesive,
paint,
brushes,
paper,
pencils,
potato,
knife,
piece of linoleum,
block of wood,
ink.

What to do
If possible, arrange a visit to your local post office. Look at the different departments or jobs, concentrating on the mail. The sorting office is particularly interesting. For more information write to the Post Office Education and Information Services, Public Relations Unit, Royal Mail House, 29 Wellington Street, Leeds LS1 1DA.

In school, set up an internal mail system. This is a particularly suitable activity for Christmas. Make a letter-box from cardboard and paint it red, then design school postage stamps. Print the design on paper using a cut potato.

Stick a piece of linoleum on to a block of wood and use a craft knife to cut a design for franking the letters.

Display the collection times, and organise teams of children to collect, sort and deliver the post to the rest of the school.

Picking it up

Age range
Nine upwards.

Group size
The whole class or group of any size.

What you need
A visit to a local garage or police pound, books, plastic bag, scrap materials for constructing levers, pivots and pulleys.

What to do
Look at the ways in which cars and vans are lifted at the garage or pound. Talk to the people working there about their methods of lifting.

In the classroom reconstruct these lifting mechanisms. By piling heavy books on top of a plastic bag, making a small opening and blowing into the bag, you can lift a surprisingly large weight. A hydraulic lift works on the same principle, but with liquid rather than air.

Experiment with levers and pivots. Where is the most effective place for a pivot? Try constructing a system of pulleys. Is it easier to lift a weight with more than one pulley? Is it easier with three? How can you show the difference in ease of lifting between the different systems?

Using toy cars and suitable materials for levers, pulleys and hydraulic lifts, construct a working model of the lifting gear in use at the garage or pound. See the activities in 'Lifts' on page 119 for further ideas.

Follow-up
Design posters about dangerous parking such as on corners, bends and pavements, or double parking.

Long distance

Age range
Seven to eleven.

Group size
The whole class.

What you need
Someone who works as a long distance lorry driver, preferably a parent or friend, pencils, paper.

What to do
Talk with the children about the job of a long distance lorry driver. Ask them to write down what they think would be a typical day for a lorry driver, including the hours worked and the distance travelled. Discuss what the children would like to find out and what sort of questions they should ask.

Invite the lorry driver into school and talk about his job. How correct were the children's estimates? Were there any surprises about the job? Look at the problems and advantages of this kind of work.

Follow-up
Using a large scale map of Britain, plot the lorry driver's routes over one week. Ask the children to write a piece of work entitled 'A day in the life of a long distance lorry driver'.

People selling things

Supermarket

Age range
Five to eleven.

Group size
The whole class divided into groups.

What you need
A supermarket. (A large supermarket with its own bakery and butcher will be more interesting than one where everything arrives ready-packaged.)

What to do
Ask the groups of children to investigate different departments such as the bakery, butcher, delicatessen, greengrocer and frozen foods. Follow the route of goods from their arrival in the supermarket through storage (children enjoy the giant freezer rooms), processing (if any), and on to the shelves. How often are goods delivered? How long is the shelf-life of various items? What happens to goods after their 'sell by' date has expired?

Follow-up
Interview people who work in the supermarket. How are their jobs organised? How long do workers spend at the check-out? What other jobs do these same people do? Who decides who does what?

Fruit and vegetables

Age range
Five to nine.

Group size
The whole class divided into groups. (The size of the group will be determined by the amount of space in the shop.)

What you need
A friendly greengrocer.

What to do
Take groups of children to visit the greengrocer's shop.
   Look at the way the fruit and vegetables are displayed. How are they arranged? How has the greengrocer made them look attractive? Is the fruit sold from the display, or from other stock in boxes underneath?

Can the children work out where the fruit and vegetables were grown, by looking at the labels on their boxes? Watch a customer buying fruit or vegetables. What do they ask for? How are the goods weighed? How does the greengrocer work out the price? (This will vary in different shops. It would be interesting to compare a well-equipped shop with a market stall.) Are the goods wrapped up? How?

Invite the greengrocer to visit the classroom and talk with the children. You could ask:
- where the greengrocer gets the fruit and vegetables from (many children will assume that they come straight from the farmer);
- how the prices are set (many children think that the greengrocer will charge the same amount as he paid; others think that the selling price will be lower because the goods are second hand);
- what the profits are used for;
- whether goods ever have to be thrown away because they have gone mouldy.

Follow-up
Set up a greengrocer's shop in your classroom. This could either be a simulation, with model fruits and vegetables made from Plasticine or papier mâché, or it could be a stall selling real fruit for children to buy and eat at playtime. The second alternative has clear advantages in that children will have to buy the fruit they are going to sell, and work out suitable selling prices.

Get the children to set out their display attractively, and to label goods. The seller will have to weigh out fruits and vegetables and charge correctly for the quantity bought.

Shoppers' choice

Age range
Seven to eleven.

Group size
Groups of four to six children.

What you need
A market, nearby shops, pencils, paper.

Interview shoppers in the market.
- Do they use the market regularly? Why (or why not?).
- What goods do they buy in the market in preference to the shops? Why?
- What goods do they buy in shops in preference to the market? Why?
- What improvements would they like to see in the market?

Follow-up
Interview stall-holders. This may be difficult; most stall-holders want to be selling, not talking to children. Try to

What to do
Ask each group of children to investigate the range and price of goods on one stall in the street market. Then visit shops and note the prices of comparable goods. Can the same goods be found in markets and shops or are there differences in type or quality of the goods sold?

choose a slack time in the market, or invite the stall-holders to school on a day the market is not open.

Find out how long they have had a stall in that market. If it is a weekly market ask them what they do on other days. Do they have to have a licence to sell in a street market? Do they have to pay to have the stall?

What shop do we need?

Age range
Seven to eleven.

Group size
The whole class divided into groups.

What you need
A small high street or shopping street with a vacant shop. If there are no vacant shops, the same activity would be possible but plan for converting a house into a shop. Clipboards, pencils, paper, felt-tipped pens.

What to do
The idea of this activity is to decide what sort of business should be set up in the vacant shop. First ask the children to make a survey of all the shops in the street (or section of the street if it is very long). Make a map of the street and classify all the different types of shops with a colour code.

Next conduct a survey among shoppers to find out what sort of business they think would be most useful in the vacant shop. This will involve asking shoppers how often they use the shopping area, whether they also shop elsewhere, and if so, for what.

Finally, ask each group of children to decide what sort of shop would be most useful and successful in the street. Carry out a planning meeting at which each group puts forward its own scheme.

Follow-up
Invite a planning officer from the local council to visit the class and explain to the children how the planning law works and what authority the council has in cases like the one the children have investigated.

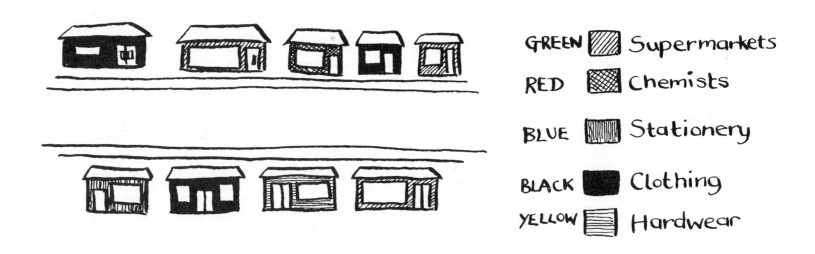

GREEN — Supermarkets
RED — Chemists
BLUE — Stationery
BLACK — Clothing
YELLOW — Hardwear

A question of profit

Age range
Seven to eleven.

Group size
About ten children.

What you need
Plastic money, objects to represent the goods that are to be traded such as Plasticine fruit and vegetables.

What to do
Get the children to take on roles as producers, transport companies, wholesalers, shopkeepers and customers. Two of each are the minimum needed; once the children understand the idea you may decide to involve the whole class at the same time.

Each person has some money, with the exception of the producer, who has all the goods. Customers receive regular pay packets.

The idea is to get the goods from the producer to the customer. But each person who handles the goods along the way will want to make a profit. The price at which the goods change hands at any stage is determined by bargaining.

Decide whether the customers are also allowed to bargain. They can't usually in this country, but they can choose to go to the cheapest shop, and everyone else in the chain can also decide to go to the cheapest seller. Children often find this activity very difficult. They tend to want to sell their goods, even at a loss, and halfway through the simulation demand extra money because they have gone broke.

At a later stage you can add complications such as a limited shelf-life for the goods.

Follow-up
Invite a local shopkeeper to talk with the class about pricing goods. Point out that overheads such as tax and rates take up part of the profit.

Shoppers' survey

Age range
Seven to eleven.

Group size
The whole class working in pairs or threes.

What you need
A local shop that is used by the children and their parents. Ask the shopkeepers in advance whether they are prepared to allow your class to carry out a consumer survey of their customers. Clipboards, pencils, paper, copies of the questionnaire on photocopiable page 125.

What to do

Discuss with the children the purpose and value of market research.

Get the children to draw up a questionnaire to use with the customers of the shop or use the market research questionnaire provided on photocopiable page 125. Ask the shopkeeper to make suggestions too. Include questions such as:

- What has been purchased?
- How often does the shopper use the shop?
- How could the shop be improved (range of goods on sale, layout, labelling etc)?

Carry out the survey. If possible take a whole day for the survey, changing groups every hour, so that differences in shopping times can be noted.

Follow-up

Analyse the results of the questionnaire. Does the time of day affect the purchases? Is it mostly men or women who are shopping? What products would the customer like to see added to the shop's selection of goods? Are the customers generally satisfied?

Draw up a chart of results of the survey, and invite the shopkeeper to visit the class to hear the children's conclusions.

Stock requisition

Age range
Nine upwards.

Group size
Pairs.

What you need
Catalogues of books and educational equipment, book and stock requisition forms, pencils.

What to do
This activity could be a real stock-ordering exercise using the profits of a class mini-enterprise; more likely, though, it will be a simulation in which the children plan for a hypothetical new class in the school.

Tell them how much money they have to spend to equip the new class. Get them to decide on their priorities, choose what they want to buy, and fill in the appropriate stock requisitions.

Follow-up
When you have the opportunity to spend some money on classroom equipment discuss with the class your priorities and decisions about spending.

Computer booking

Age range
Nine upwards.

Group size
Small groups.

What you need
A travel agency which will allow a group of children to visit and to watch work behind a counter.

What to do
Visit a local travel agency and ask the children to find out how a holiday is booked. Travel agents use computers to find out what is available, and to check all the details of intended journeys and packages.

Ask the travel agent to explain to the children how the computer is used. Find out which are the most popular holiday destinations. Do most people travel by aeroplane, boat or train? What different sorts of accommodation are available?

Follow-up
Use a data processing program on your school computer to simulate the holiday booking system used in the travel agency.

Discuss how travel agents used to make bookings before there were any computers, and before there were any telephones.

Pizzas, biscuits or buns?

Age range
Five to eleven.

Group size
The whole class.

What you need
Pencils, paper, recipe books, cooking equipment: bowls, spoons, scales, baking tins etc; ingredients for recipe, access to a stove (if you intend to go into large scale production, ask the school cook if it would be possible to use the big ovens in the school kitchens).

What to do
Set up a class enterprise producing and selling food which children in the school, staff and parents would buy.

The first step is to do market research. What sort of food would people in the school like? Look through all the suggestions and get the children to decide which ones would be practicable.

When the children have decided what they are going to produce, they will need to investigate recipes and ingredients, and to cook trial batches.

Next, the class will need to calculate the cost of ingredients and fuel for cooking, and decide how much they intend to charge. This will involve considering whether there will be any waste, and how much profit they want to make.

Before they can begin production they will need to raise the necessary capital to buy the ingredients and equipment, either through a bank loan or by each child contributing to a co-operative (see 'Start up capital' on page 81). They will also need to advertise their product (see 'Hidden persuaders' on page 82).

Decide how long the mini-enterprise is going to run; every day for two weeks? or once a week for half a term?

The children will need to decide who is going to do what in their company. Should everyone have a turn at all the jobs, or should they keep the same jobs throughout?

Finally, the children will need to decide how to spend the profit, if any.

Follow-up
Visit a fast food restaurant, a bakery or a food factory making a similar product to the one the class has produced. Having run their own company the children will be looking with an informed eye, and should find plenty to ask!

Sale!

Age range
Seven to eleven.

Group size
The whole class.

What you need
The children can decide this.

What to do
Get the class to organise a sale. They should make all the decisions themselves, as far as possible, and should use the teacher as a consultant rather than a boss.

They will need to make the following decisions:

- What are they going to do with the profit? Are they going to give it to charity? If so, which? (See 'Charity fund-raiser' on page 19.)

- What is to be sold: second-hand toys, books and clothes? Or items the class have made?
- Where are they going to get the goods from? Can they find enough themselves or do they need to ask other classes to bring things in?
- Where and when will the sale be held?
- Who is invited? Children? Parents? Outsiders?
- Will there be refreshments? If so, what? Who will provide them?
- Are there going to be any sideshows and games to make extra money? If so, what?
- How is it to be advertised? (See 'Hidden persuaders' on page 82.)
- Who is to do what job within the class?
- Do they need any capital? (See 'Start up capital' on page 81.)
- How will they organise a float of change for each stall?

Follow-up
Invite the organiser of any large scale public event to come to talk with the children about the decisions they had to make.

80

Start up capital

Age range
Nine upwards.

Group size
Small group representing class.

What you need
A bank.

What to do
The purpose of this activity is to borrow money to fund a real enterprise which the class are planning. (See, for example, 'Pizzas, biscuits or buns?' on page 78.)

Before visiting the bank make quite sure that the children fully understand why they need the money and what they will do with it. The manager will need to be convinced that the scheme will be profitable, so the children should take with them any documents they have prepared outlining their plans.

Telephone the bank and make an appointment for the children to see the manager. Explain to the manager that the purpose of the activity is for the children to learn about raising capital, and that it would be helpful if he or she could ask them questions in the same way as enquiries would be made about an adult loan.

Take the group to visit the bank and ask for a loan. They may have to go to more than one bank. Are interest rates the same everywhere?

Consider alternative methods of raising capital for your class enterprise. What about having a co-operative structure in which all the children contribute equally? Would it be possible to sell shares?

Follow-up
Having raised the necessary capital, the class can run their enterprise. They will need to keep accurate accounts, and to meet regularly to make decisions about spending the capital, pricing goods or services, and deciding what to do with the profit, if any.

Hidden persuaders

Age range
Seven to eleven.

Group size
The whole class divided into groups.

What you need
Advertisements from newspapers and magazines, video recorder, tape recorder, camera, a product, service or event to advertise, large sheets of paper, paint, brushes, felt-tipped pens.

What to do
This activity forms part of a class mini-enterprise: for example 'Pizzas, biscuits or buns?' on page 78.

Ask the children to make a collection of magazine and newspaper advertisements for products similar to their own.

Compile tapes of radio and television advertisements. Photograph street posters and advertisement hoardings.

Discuss how each of these advertisements is trying to make the product appeal to the public. Do the children think that all the claims made are honest?

Decide what are the selling points of your product or service which should be emphasised in advertisements. Decide how much information should go in the advertisements. Some advertising campaigns start by disclosing very little information, and aim to whet the public's curiosity.

Ask groups of children to work out possible advertising campaigns for the class product, service or event.

Discuss all the ideas with the whole class and choose the best ideas. Carry them out. These could include:
- a continuous loop of video tape to put in the school entrance hall;
- commercial breaks in assemblies;
- a poster campaign;
- taped 'radio' advertisements to play at the end of assembly or playtime.

Follow-up
Invite someone who works in an advertising agency to visit the class and talk about their job and other jobs in advertising.

Best buy

Age range
Nine upwards.

Group size
Groups of three or four children.

What you need
Copies of *Which?* magazine, different brands of ball-point pens, pieces of fabric, washing powder, pencils, paper, copies of the chart on photocopiable page 126.

What to do
Introduce the idea of consumer testing to the class, and let them look at copies of *Which?* magazine. These should give them some ideas about fair tests, and layout of results.

Explain that each group is to test a product and produce a report advising consumers which brand is the 'best buy'.

Children should devise their own tests. If they get stuck you could suggest those given here and provide the children with a copy of the chart on photocopiable page 126.

- If you subject the pen to heat (a radiator) or cold (a refrigerator) will it still write?
- If you get the ink on clothing, how easy is it to get out?
- Is the line produced of good quality – even and continuous?
- How much pressure is needed to write?
- Does the pen produce messy blobs of ink from time to time?
- Is the design attractive?
- How long will the pen write for?

- If the cap is left off for a week, does the pen still write?

When the groups have tested all the pens, ask them to write a report of their findings and, taking the price into consideration, recommend a 'best buy'.

Follow-up
Publish reports of the children's findings in the school or class magazine.

People entertaining people

A career in football

Age range
Seven to eleven.

Group size
The whole class.

What you need
A local professional football club. You are more likely to be successful if you approach a club in the third or fourth division which does not have so many demands upon it. You do not need to meet the club's first team; it would be equally interesting to meet apprentices.

What to do
If possible, arrange a visit to the club's training ground. Otherwise invite players, apprentices or other workers to visit the school to talk with the children about their routine and work.

Young children often assume that footballers are not paid for their work; they are enjoying playing a game and must have other jobs to support themselves.

Follow-up
Find out about training and career opportunities in other sports.

Stage-struck

Age range
Seven to eleven.

Group size
Small groups.

What you need
A visit to a theatre, tape recorders, clipboards, paper, pencils, cameras.

What to do
Organise groups of children to spend time with different workers in the theatre. Let the children watch them work and ask questions about their jobs. For example, they could investigate the ticket office, finance, the wardrobe, lighting, design, creation and painting of scenery, stage management, sound effects and the restaurant or cafeteria.

Ask them to record the routine of a typical day, investigate the equipment used, and find out how this work contributes to the production.

Follow-up
Set up a theatre company in your classroom. Ask the children to take on all the different jobs, and organise a performance for the rest of the school or for parents.

Arrange a class visit to a performance at the theatre.

Books to borrow

Age range
Nine upwards.

Group size
Large groups.

What you need
Your local public library and a co-operative librarian.

What to do
Find out about the work of the librarian. What is the daily routine in the library? Who decides which books to buy, and which ones to discard? Where does the money come from? How are the books organised and what sort of catalogue is kept? What sort of records of loans are kept? What other jobs do librarians do?

Follow-up
The children could look at the school or class library. Are the books clearly organised and labelled? Is it easy for children to locate the books they need? What kind of records are kept of books or their use?

What improvements can the children suggest as a result of their investigations at the public library? (For example, colour coding and symbols might be helpful for some children.) Carry out the improvements that the class agrees on.

Planning for leisure

Age range
Seven to eleven.

Group size
The whole class organised into groups.

What you need
Information about local leisure facilities (you can often get these from the public library), clipboards, paper, pencils.

What to do
Choose a plot of land near the school which could be developed for leisure facilities. (It could be part of your school playground. This would cause more controversy, as the children would have to argue the relative merits of the existing playground or a new facility.)

Make a survey of existing leisure facilities in your area. Then interview local children and adults to find out what new facilities they would like on the site (theatre, swimming pool, ice rink etc).

Ask groups of children to draw up plans for the most popular suggestions. Invite an architect, or people who work in local leisure facilities, to advise and comment on the plans.

Follow-up
Carry out a planning enquiry in the school. Ask groups of children to present evidence for and against the different potential uses of the site. Ask an adult (maybe a parent) to act as a planning inspector.

Looking after animals

Age range
Five to nine.

Group size
Whole class to visit, follow-up in groups.

What you need
Any workplace where animals are cared for such as a riding school, a farm, a zoo, a pet shop, a stable for police horses or a dogs' home.

What to do
Visit any workplace where animals are looked after.

Interview the people who work with the animals and find out about the daily routine. What do the animals

eat? Where does the food come from? How is it prepared? How often are the animals fed? What about cleaning them out? Do they have to be exercised?

Think also about seasonal jobs such as sheep-shearing or looking after the young.

Why are the animals kept? Do they work? Are they there as a tourist attraction? Who pays for looking after them?

Follow-up
Write books on caring for classroom and household pets. Children could work in groups, sharing their ideas about the care of each type of animal.

Try hatching out chicken or duck eggs in the classroom. (Fertilised eggs can often be bought from farms, and incubators can sometimes be borrowed from farms or secondary schools.)

Run a zoo in the classroom (see 'Classroom zoo' on page 90).

Classroom zoo

Age range
Five to nine.

Group size
The whole class.

What you need
Children's own small pet animals in suitable cages or containers eg rabbits, hamsters, guinea pigs, mice, gerbils, tortoises, goldfish, stick-insects, classroom pets; minibeasts the class have collected (a wormery, tadpoles etc), pencils, paper, felt-tipped pens, books on pet care, orange squash, biscuits.

What to do
Run a zoo in your classroom for one day. Plan the day well in advance, and write to parents explaining what is going to happen. You need to make sure that they do not send in large pets; a classroom full of dogs and cats would be chaotic!

  Before the Zoo Day ask the children to write about their own pets. Pictures and books about animals could also be displayed. Make posters and display them around the school. Invite other classes to visit the zoo.

  On the day, arrange the whole classroom as a zoo. Organise the children to take it in turns to do different jobs such as taking money at the door; showing their visitors around or selling refreshments.

Follow-up
Organise a class visit to your nearest zoo.

Music and dance

Age range
Seven to eleven.

Group size
Large group or whole class.

What you need
A professional dancer or musician. You do not need a famous performer, but rather anyone who earns their living through music or dancing – someone in the chorus, an orchestra player or a session musician. A male dancer would help to counter sex-role stereotyping. Paper, pencils.

What to do
Invite the dancer or musician to visit your class and talk with children about their training and work. Younger children often class the work of performers as a hobby and are uncertain whether they are paid for it. They also tend to think only about the glamorous aspects of the work, and to ignore the long hours of practice, inconvenient working hours, and uncertain employment prospects.

Ask your visitor to talk about these aspects, as well as the satisfactions of the job.

Get the children to list the advantages and disadvantages of the different jobs they have learnt about.

Follow-up
Visit a theatre or dancing school to watch a rehearsal.

Some theatres and music companies run schemes for schools to adopt a dancer or musician. Make enquiries about involving your class in such a scheme.

Swimming pool

Age range
Nine upwards.

Group size
Small groups.

What you need
A local swimming pool, paper, pencils, felt-tipped pens.

What to do
Investigate the range of jobs at your local swimming pool. Who takes the money? Who is responsible for cleaning? Who decides who does what? Does the same building house other services such as a laundry, public baths or gymnasium? Are these administered separately, or is one person in charge of everything?

Get different groups of children to interview different workers about their jobs, to build up an overall picture of the division of labour and the interactions between the workers.

Make a large diagram showing the different groups of workers and indicating the relationships between them, such as 'gives orders to', 'gives information to', 'gives advice to' and so on.

Follow-up
Investigate the financial and administrative links between the swimming pool and other groups in the community such as the Council, rate payers, the Local Education Authority, swimming pool users and the local swimming club.

If the swimming pool also houses a laundry, suggestions for activities are given in 'Keeping Clean' on page 103.

Writing for money

Age range
Five to eleven.

Group size
The whole class.

What you need
A friendly local author. A writer of children's books would be ideal, but they tend to be very much in demand. Try your local college of education or polytechnic, or the LEA language adviser may be able to put you in touch with someone. The Book Trust may also be able to help; the address to write to is Book House, 45 East Hill, Wandsworth, London SW18 2QZ.

What to do
Invite the author to visit your classroom to talk with the children about her work. Discuss with the children beforehand what they want to find out.

These are areas which could be included:
- How is a working day spent? (Many authors do other jobs as well.)
- Does the author write with pen and paper, a typewriter or a word processor? Why?
- How and when was the publisher contacted? What sort of contract was arranged? When does the author get paid?
- What are proofs? What does the author do with them? Perhaps they could bring some proofs to show the class.

Follow-up
Invite a publisher to visit the class to talk about the work involved in producing a book or magazine.

Ask the children to write, produce and sell their own books of stories and poems.

Eating out

Age range
Nine upwards.

Group size
The whole class.

What you need
One or more local eating places, preferably of different types, for example, cafe, snack bar, restaurant; clipboards, paper, pencils.

What to do
Discuss 'eating out' with the children. Arrange visits to one or more different places. Find out about the variation in prices, variety of food, opening hours, atmosphere, and so on.

Talk to the staff about their jobs. Interview a selection of different workers; waitresses and washers-up as well as managers. What are the advantages and disadvantages of the different jobs? Which jobs would the children like to do? Who makes the decisions? What happens if there is a disagreement? Do the workers belong to a union?

In class talk about what the children have found out. Divide the class into groups and get the children to enact an incident that might arise in one of the eating places – a complaint by a customer about the food or the bill, a row between a waiter and a customer about a tip and so on.

Follow-up
Set up a mini-enterprise in the classroom. This is outlined in 'Pizza, biscuits or buns?' on page 78.

Illustration and design

Age range
Five to eleven.

Group size
The whole class.

What you need
An artist or graphic designer (you may be able to contact one through the *Yellow Pages*); a range of drawing and painting materials, lettering pens etc.

What to do
Ask the children to design and illustrate books of their own stories. Invite an artist or graphic designer to join the class to advise them about their ideas and help them to carry them out. It would be helpful if the artist/designer could bring his own current work into the classroom to discuss it with the class and demonstrate artwork techniques.

Alternatively you could invite the designer to help the children with a project to improve labelling and lettering on displays and notices throughout the school.

Follow-up
If possible visit the artist or designer in their studio or workplace.

TV consumer survey

Age range
Nine upwards.

Group size
The whole class working individually, then in small groups.

What you need
Copies of *Radio Times* and *TV Times* to give a complete record of programmes for the week, pens and squared paper for graphs. You may also want to use a computer with a data processing program.

What to do
Ask the children to keep a record of all the television programmes they watch during one week.

Divide the class into small groups to collect the results. Record them on graphs showing how many children watched each programme and how many hours of television each child watched. They will have to decide whether to include programmes which they only watched in part.

If a computer is available a data processing program could be used, rather than drawing graphs.

Follow-up
Ask the children to write reviews of the programmes they most enjoyed during the week.

Send all the results to the appropriate television company, together with the children's suggestions for improving the service.

Listen before you speak!

Age range
Seven to eleven.

Group size
Whole class.

What you need
A circle of chairs.

What to do
This exercise encourages children to listen carefully to what is said, and to base their questions on what they hear, rather than on a precise list drawn up beforehand.

Explain that TV chat show hosts think carefully about what sort of questions they will ask their guests before the show, but change the questions they actually ask as the guest talks to them. They have to listen carefully, and think as they listen. The class are now going to interview you about your job, but every question must arise from the answer to the previous question. Warn them that your answers might not be what they expect!

Make your answers as bizarre as possible. Answer the question, but be deliberately inconsistent, try to get off the point and give unexpected replies. This can be an amusing lesson for everyone, and children soon enter the game of listening carefully to check that every question really does follow on from your answers. You could vary the game by pointing to the child who must ask the next question.

Everyone is kept on their toes with this – including you!

An exchange might go like this:

Child: Do you enjoy your work?
Teacher: Only at the weekends.
Child: Why the weekends?
Teacher: That's when I'm not working.
Child: But . . . why don't you like your work?
Teacher: I can't stand children.
Child: But if you can't stand children, why did you choose to become a teacher?
Teacher: I didn't choose, my Dad chose for me.
Child: How could he make you be a teacher?
Teacher: He didn't.
Child: But you just said . . .

Follow-up
Try a session when you consistently try to evade answering the question. Can they pin you down?

People helping people

Helping people

Age range
Five to seven.

Group size
The whole class.

What you need
A corner of the classroom with suitable furniture for simulating a health centre: beds, chairs, table etc. Stethoscope, notebook and pencil, toys, scissors, bandages. A visit from a local health centre staff member.

What to do
Most children have visited their doctor or health centre at some time. Talk to the children about their experiences and/or invite someone from your local health centre to come into the school. Whom have they met at the health centre? What were these people doing? Ask the children to say what they think the nurses, doctors, receptionists, and anyone else they have met do.

Help the children to organise their home corner into a health centre. Ask the children to act out the roles of patients and staff.

Follow-up
Visit the health centre, and if possible talk to some of the staff about their jobs. In school, look at the differences between what the children thought the people did and what they actually saw. Draw large pictures of people working at the health centre, and write about their different jobs. Don't forget people like cleaners, caretakers and night emergency staff. Invite someone from the health centre to see your display. When you have finished with it offer it to the health centre for display in their waiting room.

On the ward

Age range
Nine upwards.

Group size
The whole class or group of any size.

What you need
A contact with a local hospital, pencils, pens, paper, pieces of cheese, fruit and bread, microscope.

What to do
Arrange for the children to visit the hospital to see the work of several departments.

In the classroom, carry out a range of activities that follow on from your visit. For example, if you visit the children's ward, the children might design a playroom suitable for sick children; if you meet the dietician, the children could draw up plans for a healthy diet.

Other ideas include studying germs and growing cultures. Try leaving pieces of cheese, fruit and bread in the classroom and examine the moulds that grow on them. Expose the foods to different conditions: dry, damp, warm, cold etc, and note the variations in growth of moulds. Borrow a microscope and examine the moulds in more detail.

Follow-up
Ask the children to design machines to help patients with particular problems. They could design special gadgets, such as a bread-holder, a page-turner or something to help a person get out of the bath. Show the work to some of the people you met at the hospital. Ask them for their opinions.

Save trees

Age range
Seven to eleven.

Group size
The whole class.

What you need
Lots of old newspapers, several buckets of water, a sink or bowl, clean yoghurt or margarine tubs, paper, pens, old plates, petroleum jelly, paints, brushes, clear varnish.

What to do
Ask the children how their families get rid of old newspapers. Do they burn the paper or throw it in the bin? Some may take their paper to a recycling plant.

Put some water in the buckets. Tear up old newspapers into shreds and soak them in the water. Stir the mixture until it is well-soaked. Working over a sink or a bowl, take out handfuls of the paper pulp and fill the margarine tubs. Press the mixture down, squeezing out as much water as possible. Leave the tubs to drain over the sink. When the paper pulp is well-drained, empty the tubs carefully on to a wad of newspaper and allow the pulp to dry out completely. It will dry out more quickly if placed somewhere warm, such as close to a radiator.

Advertise and sell the brickettes to home-owners with open fires. (This should not be attempted in smokeless zones.)

Alternatively, make items from papier mâché. Collect together some old plates. Cover one side with petroleum jelly and build up several layers of papier mâché. When they are dry, carefully remove the papier mâché plates. Decorate them with paints and cover them with a layer of clear varnish. Advertise and sell the paper plates.

Follow-up
Get the children to devise some tests to find out the different qualities of newsprint. They could test for absorbency (which paper is best for wrapping fish and chips?), for ink permanence (on which paper could you dry a jumper without the printer's ink staining the clothes?) or for strength (which paper will hold the greatest weight?).

Ask the children to test the relative strengths of different newspapers. Cut sheets from different newspapers to the same size and make bridges from them to test which is the strongest.

Experiment with different ways of folding the paper. If the children roll the paper tightly they will be able to make a very strong structure. Which group can make the tallest structure?

No ball games

Age range
Seven to eleven.

Group size
The whole class or groups of six or more.

What you need
A convenient local park, paper, pencils, pens, graph paper.

What to do
Spend some time in your local park. Look at the people working in the park. What sort of jobs are they doing? What other jobs need to be done? Who delivers the food for the cafeteria? Who clears away all the rubbish? Where do all the new young plants come from and who grows them? In the classroom draw up a list of the different people required to keep the park in good condition.

Look at the different types of people who use the park such as elderly people or children. Visit the park again and make a survey of the people you see in the park. Try to do this at different times during the day.

In the classroom, make a graph showing the various groups using the park and discuss the different needs. For example, is there a need for spaces for ball games, for the elderly, for small children or for dogs?

Follow-up
Set up a role-play exercise. Divide the children into the following groups: children, parents with small children, elderly people, football players and park workers.

Tell them that the park is going to be redesigned. Ask each group to submit a design to make it a better place for their group. Hold a public meeting in which each group can put forward their case for improved facilities. Invite another class, or a group from another class, to listen to the debate and to help with the decision making. Then design a park that will please (nearly) everyone.

Keeping clean

Age range
Seven to eleven.

Group size
The whole class or group of about eight.

What you need
A laundrette, local laundry or baths with laundry facilities, washing powder, paper, pencils.

What to do
Discuss the processes which are involved in washing clothes: soaking, washing, rubbing, scrubbing, rinsing, spinning, drying, ironing, pressing and so on.

Invite any parents or grandparents who remember old-fashioned ways of washing to talk to the children about copper boilers, washboards, flat-irons etc. Compare the different ways of washing then and now. Was it harder work then? Who generally did the washing? Who generally does the washing in your home today? Try washing some items using washboards and bars of soap.

Put some heavy items in the wash and let the children feel the weight of wet washing. Weigh a towel dry and wet and see how much the water weighs.

Carry out a variety of tests on a number of different fabrics; test for shrinkage, stretching, colour fastness etc. Encourage the children to identify and devise the tests that are needed. Emphasise the need for fair tests and accurate recording. Try washing garments made dirty with the same quantities of oil, tomato ketchup, grass stains etc in different temperatures and different powders (eg biological, detergent, soap flakes, stain removers). Show the results in chart form. When parents are doing the washing, does this count as work?

Follow-up
See also 'Swimming pool' on page 92.

Look at the washing instruction labels in clothes. How clear are they? Design some alternative labels. Test them out on some other classes. Do they understand your symbols?

Test out some of the washing aids on the market, those which claim to remove stains etc. Devise fair tests. Do their claims stand up to testing? Go on to consider advertisements for washing products.

School signposts

Age range
Five to nine.

Group size
The whole class.

What you need
Paper, paints, brushes.

What to do
Arrange for the children to interview and draw portraits of all the staff in the school: the teachers, schoolkeeper, support staff, part time teachers and cleaners. Display the portraits in the entrance hall for parents and visitors.

What do visitors need to know about the building? Where are the toilets, the head's room and the secretary's office. Get them to design pictorial signs to identify the headteacher's room, the schoolkeeper's room and so on.

Follow-up
Choose to look at a specific job that is done in the school. You might choose the schoolkeeper's job. What do the children think the schoolkeeper does? Arrange for a small group to interview the schoolkeeper. If possible record the interview on tape. Report back to the rest of the class. Can the children suggest ways of making the job easier – by picking up litter, or avoiding damage to the premises? Present the ideas in assembly and try to develop a school policy. Act out a scene to show some of the problems of being the schoolkeeper.

Go on to look at another job, perhaps that of the secretary.

School information

Age range
Seven to eleven.

Group size
The whole class.

What you need
Computer, paper, pencils, felt-tipped pens.

What to do
Arrange to visit other classes in the school and interview both the teachers and the children to find out what activities they do in each class such as swimming, clubs, or after-school events. Find out what activities become available as the children progress through the school. Find out about play centres, sports teams, school journey opportunities etc. Make up a booklet of information for new pupils. Use the word processing programme on the computer and lay out the information attractively with illustrations.

Follow-up
Carry out a survey in the school asking children to remember what it was like to be a new pupil. Are there ways in which new pupils could be made to feel more welcome? Display the results of the survey in a place where everyone can read them, or announce the results in the school assembly.

Dinner time

Age range
Nine upwards.

Group size
Small group, then whole class.

What you need
A helpful school cook, paper, pencils.

What to do
Arrange for the children to interview the school cook about her work. Ask her how she plans her menus, orders the right quantities, organises the staff, and so on. Visit the cook in the kitchen, and if possible, invite her to the classroom to talk about her work.

Follow-up
Ask the children what meals they would like to have at school. Plan a week's menus and try to work out the amounts of food that would be needed to feed the whole class. Draw up a chart giving the details. Represent the figures in a pictorial chart: so many sacks of flour, sugar, packets of margarine etc. Work out the quantities needed for the whole school and make a second chart. Ask the cook to look at the charts and give her comments. Compare the two charts.

Carry out a survey on the children's favourite school dinners.

Make a cake and present it to the cook.

Throw away

Age range
Seven to eleven.

Group size
The whole class.

What you need
A collection of throw-away items eg cardboard boxes, string, empty drink cans, newspapers, fabrics, plastic bags and cartons, empty bottles; tongs, bowls of sand, trowel, matches, hammer, protective goggles, copies of the chart on photocopiable page 127.

What to do
Ask the children to bring in some items from their rubbish bins (clean, unbroken items only). Sort the items into groups according to the materials from which they are made; eg glass, tin, fabric, plastic etc. Devise tests for the materials to find out how easy or difficult it is to dispose of each item. Record the results on the chart on photocopiable page 127. Will it rot? Bury it in the ground for a set period of time. Will it melt or burn? Try burning a small square of each fabric. (Take safety precautions by holding the material with a pair of tongs over a bowl of sand, and having an adult to supervise at all times. Have plenty of fresh air in the classroom.) Try compacting it into a very small area by crushing it with a hammer (protect the eyes with goggles).

Follow-up
Visit a rubbish tip and talk to the people who work there, or ask someone from your local council cleansing department to come into the school and talk to the children about rubbish disposal. What materials cause the greatest problems? Which things can be recycled and used again? Which are the most dangerous for humans or for animals? What are the dangers of the job for the refuse-collectors? Can the children think of ways of helping to keep the school tidier?

Ask the children to bring a selection of scrap materials into school and make models from it.

See also 'Save trees' on page 101.

Clean teeth

Age range
Seven to eleven.

Group size
The whole class.

What you need
A visit from the school dentist or dental nurse, plaque display tablets, a number of small mirrors, red crayons.

What to do
Invite your school dentist or dental nurse into the classroom to talk to the children. Ask her to talk about her job and to discuss the importance of caring for teeth.

Ask the children to bring their toothbrushes and toothpaste to school.

Let the children look at their teeth in a mirror, and then draw the teeth as they see them.

Ask the children to clean their teeth then chew plaque display tablets. Next allow each child to look at his mouth in the mirror so that they can see the amount of plaque that they have on their teeth. Ask them to colour the plaque in red on their drawings.

Follow-up
Carry out a survey of the number of times children throughout the school clean their teeth, the number of sweets they eat and how many fillings they have.

Emergency!

Age range
Seven to eleven.

Group size
The whole class.

What you need
A visit from one of the emergency services.

What to do
All children are excited by fire engines, police cars and ambulances. Some of them have had direct experience of emergencies. Discuss with the children the role of the emergency services. When do you need them? How do you call them? What do the different services do?

Arrange for a visitor from one of the emergency services to come into the school to talk to the children about their work. They often have a good range of educational material for schools.

Follow-up
Using a toy telephone, simulate your own emergency services. On a series of cards, write down some possible emergencies: a car accident in which one person is trapped in her seat and two are injured; an old man has fallen over in his home and cannot get up; a burglary in a jeweller's shop, and so on. Put in plenty of detail. Ask one group of children to take the cards in turn and to dial the 999 calls, while the other answers the telephone and decides which service should deal with the emergency.

This activity can be expanded, with one group of children acting out the drama, and another taking on the roles of the emergency services involved. Afterwards, get the children to discuss their roles. What special strengths does each role demand?

Look both ways

Age range
Seven to eleven.

Group size
The whole class.

What you need
A local road safety officer or the school police officer, felt-tipped pens, paints, brushes, paper.

What to do
Organise a visit from either the road safety officer or the school police officer. Ask him or her to talk to the children about road safety and, in particular, about his or her role in preventing accidents.

Get the children to design posters to display around the school warning others about the dangers on the roads.

Follow-up
Ask the children to make finger or glove puppets then devise and stage a puppet play about road safety for the younger children in the school.

Making work easier

Cleaning equipment

Age range
Seven to eleven.

Group size
Small groups.

What you need
Four squares of carpet, or a carpet marked with tape into four equal parts, small packet of flour, vacuum cleaner, carpet sweeper, dustpan and stiff brush.

What to do
Scatter equal quantities of flour on each of the four squares of carpet. Trample the flour well into each square.

Clean three squares using the different pieces of equipment, then ask the children to improvise a method for cleaning the fourth square. (If it is a separate square of carpet which can be lifted up, they might try banging it against a wall outdoors.)

Measure the time spent cleaning each square. Can the children think of any way of measuring the energy they have used?

Compare the squares of carpet? Are they all equally clean? If not, why not?

What can be concluded from the results of this activity?

Follow-up
Investigate the history of cleaning appliances and the links between their development and household furnishings; employment of servants and women's employment outside the home.

Invite some elderly people to visit the class and ask them how housework was done when they were young.

Scissors

Age range
Seven to eleven.

Group size
The whole class or small groups.

What you need
Old magazines and a pair of scissors for each child, a range of simple household tools eg can-opener, whisk, screwdriver, different types of bottle-openers, hand-drill; paper, adhesive, rulers, pencils, felt-tipped pens, books, two strips of card of equal length for each child, paper-fasteners, matchboxes, pliers.

What to do
Give the children some old magazines. Ask them to find pictures of machines that help people to work. They should be able to find, for example, lawnmowers, vacuum cleaners, vans, washing machines, bicycles, fax machines etc. Ask them to cut out one or two pictures each and then look at them together. Add a few of your own to ensure a variety. Can the children think of a way of classifying them? (Household, modern technology and transport are some possibilities.) When they have decided on their categories, stick the pictures on to large pieces of paper under headings showing how the groups are organised.

Talk to the children about the scissors they have been using. These are 'machines' too. Look at the way they work. Show the children the tools you have collected.

Let the children try the following experiments:

- Using a ruler on a pencil as a lever, work out the best position for the pivot, or fulcrum (the pencil under the ruler) for lifting a textbook.

- Simulate the action of a pair of scissors by joining two strips of card with a paper-fastener. Ask the children whether the position of the pivot has any effect on the movement of the scissors. Some children might like to make multiple scissors and see how far they can reach.
- Try pinching a matchbox. Now try again with the pliers. Notice the small amount of pressure needed when the pliers are used.

Follow-up
Look at screw mechanisms and cogs on a variety of machines. Look at all the different parts of a bicycle. Make detailed drawings of some of the parts of a bicycle. Make working models in cardboard, using cogs, pivots and levers.

Working dogs

Age range
Five to nine.

Group size
The whole class or groups.

What you need
A visit from a working dog and its owner or handler, for example a guide-dog, a police dog, a sheep dog or a guard dog.

What to do
Before meeting the working dog and its handler, the children could discuss what they already know about working dogs, and what they would like to find out.

They might like to ask, for example:
- Why do dogs work?
- Can any variety of dog work, or only certain breeds?
- What skills do dogs use in their work?
- Why are dogs used rather than people or machines? Could people or machines do these jobs?
- Is it likely that with technological advances dogs will cease to work?
- What precise job is done by the dog the children will meet?
- Could the dog work without its handler?
- How are dogs trained for different kinds of work?
- Are they paid for the work they do?
- Are there any laws protecting working dogs from exploitation and ill-treatment?

Arrange for the dog and its handler to come into school, or arrange for the class to visit them at work. Ask the handler for a demonstration of the dog's work, and to talk with the children and answer their questions.

Follow-up
Find out from books or from visits about dogs doing different types of work.

Find out about other animals that work.

Working horses

Age range
Seven to eleven.

Group size
Pairs or small groups.

What you need
An elderly person who is happy to reminisce; books about the history of transport.

What to do
Ask the children to find out whether there are any working horses in the neighbourhood. If there are, what work do they do?

Invite an elderly person into school to talk with the children about the work of horses 60 years ago. What sort of work did they do?

Research the work horses did in the last century. Why are there fewer working horses today?

Follow-up
Arrange a visit to any stables in your neighbourhood, such as police, army, riding or racehorse stables.

Spreading the load

Age range
Seven to eleven.

Group size
The whole class.

What you need
Weights with handles, long nails, cotton reels, string, dowelling, heavy books, spring balance.

What to do
Try lifting up weights from the floor using a pulley.

Make a pulley by pushing a nail through a cotton reel and attaching pieces of string to either end of the nail. Tie the pieces of string to the dowelling, making sure that the cotton reel can turn freely (see figure 1).

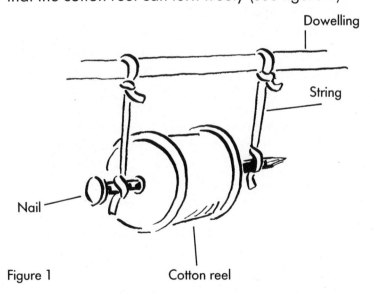

Figure 1

Nail

Cotton reel

String

Dowelling

Place the dowelling rod between two tables and weigh the ends down with heavy books to stop it slipping off. Take another piece of string and tie it to the weight and pass it over the cotton reel. Pull down on the string to lift the weight (see figure 2). Is it easier? How much?

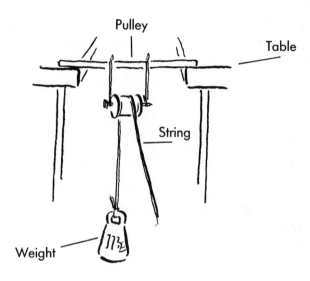

Pulley

Table

String

Weight

Figure 2

Use the spring balance to test the force needed to lift the weight without the pulley.

Follow-up
Look at pictures of people working on a building site, or look at a building site itself. How often are pulleys used?

117

Cranes

Age range
Seven to eleven.

Group size
The whole class or groups of two or three.

What you need
Pictures of cranes for reference, washing-up liquid bottles, sharp knife, yoghurt pots, string, two pieces of dowelling 30 cm in length for each child, sticky tape, marbles or conkers, paper, pens.

What to do
Talk about cranes and the jobs they do. If possible, look at some cranes in action and study the pictures of cranes.

Get the children to make cranes from washing-up liquid bottles. Using a sharp knife, cut a slit in the bottle about one third of the way down, and two more slits opposite each other at the bottom of the bottle (see figure 1). It is probably best if the teacher does the cutting.

Figure 1

Make a bucket by cutting a hole below the rim of a yoghurt pot and threading string through to make a handle. Fix this on to the end of one of the dowelling rods with string or tape, and push the rod into the bottle through the higher slit.

Figure 2

Load the bucket with marbles or conkers until the crane topples over. Encourage the children to think of ways of making it more stable, such as weighting the crane down by putting marbles in the bottom of the bottle or adding outriggers by pushing the second piece of dowelling through the slits at the bottom of the bottle (see figure 2).

Which crane can support the greatest weight? Make a chart of the results and display the cranes.

Follow-up
Look at the activity 'Spreading the load' which uses pulleys on page 117. Get the children to devise a crane combined with a pulley and see which design can lift the greatest weight.

Lifts

Age range
Seven to eleven.

Group size
The whole class.

What you need
Some heavy books, small plastic bin liners.

What to do
Sit a child on the pile of heavy books and ask the class how they could move her without straining themselves. Ask the child to stand up, then place a small plastic bin liner under the pile of books and get one of the children to blow into the bag, taking care not to let the air escape again as he blows. The pile of books will move upwards.

Ask the child to sit on the books again. Repeat the activity. The child who is blowing will be able to lift up the other child too.

Follow-up
Arrange a visit to a garage to watch a hydraulic lift in operation. See activities in 'Picking it up' on page 66.

Writing machines

Age range
Seven to eleven.

Group size
Large groups or whole class.

What you need
A variety of writing tools such as a quill pen, dip pen, fountain pen, ball-point pen, typewriter, word processor.

What to do
Ask the children to look closely at all the writing tools that you have collected together, and to consider the advantages and disadvantages of each. Try writing with them all, and discuss the differences.

Invite the school secretary or any trained typist to visit the class to demonstrate the speed possible on a typewriter or word processor, and to talk with the children about the problems and capabilities of each.

Follow-up
Investigate the workings of each tool and machine. For example, look to see how a typewriter produces the letters; does a word processor work in the same way? Find out about the history of writing tools and machines.

Copying machines

Age range
Seven to eleven.

Group size
Small groups.

What you need
Tracing paper, carbon paper, a spirit copier, an ink copier, a photocopier.

What to do
Investigate the different methods of making copies and consider the advantages and disadvantages of each.

How much does each method cost? How many copies can you make by each method? Compare the quality of the copies; which method produces the best quality?

Follow-up
Visit a local printer or invite a print worker to visit the classroom to talk to the children about other methods of duplicating material.

Investigate the history of making copies and printing.

Labour-saving gadgets

Age range
Nine upwards.

Group size
Pairs.

What you need
Paper and pencils, a collection of junk materials: wood, metal, wire, cardboard etc; a selection of tools, adhesive.

What to do
Ask each pair of children to do one of the following activities:
- Think up some labour-saving device which they would find useful, maybe to do a job they dislike doing.
- Interview parents or other adults to find out what kind of device they would find useful.
- Simply think of something that someone somewhere might find useful.

Design and draw up plans for their invention. Make a model of it or, if possible, make the real thing and try using it!

Follow-up
Ask each pair to find out about one labour-saving invention that particularly interests them. When was it first invented? What improvements have been made since the idea was first thought up?

Reproducible material

Job application form

Name: _____

Date of birth: _____

Sex: M ☐   F ☐

Address: _____
_____
_____

tel: _____

Educational qualifications:
Good school subjects: _____
_____

Other: _____

Other qualifications (secretarial etc): _____
_____

Previous employment:

Name of employer	Position held	From – to	Reason for leaving

Hobbies and interests: _____
_____
_____

Reasons for wanting this job:

[   ]

Passenger questionnaire

Point of departure _____
Where are you going? _____
How long does your journey take? _____
How many miles are you going? _____

How often do you use this route?
Daily ☐
More than once a week ☐
Less than once a week ☐
Infrequently ☐

What is the purpose of your trip?
Work ☐
School ☐
Shopping ☐
Other ☐

Do you take other journeys by bus?
Yes ☐
No ☐

What improvements would you like to see in the bus station facilities and bus service? _____

Are the buses usually on time?
Late? ☐
Early? ☐
Don't know? ☐

Are the buses busy? Do you get a seat?
Always ☐
Usually ☐
Never ☐

Passenger details
Sex: M ☐   F ☐

Age range:
Child ☐
Adult ☐
OAP ☐

Market research

What has been purchased?
Food ☐
Toiletries ☐
Domestic utensils/cleaning materials ☐
Stationery/newspapers/magazines ☐
Other _____

How often do you use this shop?
Daily ☐
Several times a week ☐
Weekly ☐
Infrequently ☐

Have you chosen to shop here because the shop is:
Nearest? ☐
Has the best range of items? ☐
Friendly service? ☐
Cheapest? ☐

What would you like to see improved about this shop?
Range of goods ☐
Layout ☐
Service ☐

Do you pay for your purchases by:
Cash? ☐
Cheque? ☐
Credit card? ☐

Personal details
Sex: M ☐   F ☐

Occupation: _____

Age range:
Child ☐
Adult ☐
OAP ☐

Best buy, see page 83

Ball-point pens Brand:	Will the pen write at extreme temperatures? Hot	Cold	Can stains be removed? How?	How good is the quality of the line? Are there messy blobs? Is the pen easy to use?	Will the pen still write if the cap is left off for: Hour? Day? Week?			How attractive is the design? ★ ★★ ★★★		
1										
2										
3										
4										
5										
6										

Throw away, see page 108

Substance Method of disposal	Cardboard	Newspapers	String	Fabrics	Empty cans	Plastic bags	Plastic cartons	Empty bottles
Bury in ground								
Burn								
Melt								
Crush								
Recycle								

Other Scholastic books

Bright Ideas
The *Bright Ideas* books provide a wealth of resources for busy primary school teachers. There are now more than 20 titles published, providing clearly explained and illustrated ideas on topics ranging from *Writing* and *Maths Activities* to *Environmental Studies* and *Christmas Art and Craft*. Each book contains material which can be photocopied for use in the classroom.

Teacher Handbooks
The *Teacher Handbooks* give an overview of the latest research in primary education, and show how it can be put into practice in the classroom. Covering all the core areas of the curriculum, the *Teacher Handbooks* are indispensable to the new teacher as a source of information and useful to the experienced teacher as a quick reference guide.

Management Books
The *Management Books* are designed to help teachers to organise their time, classroom and teaching more efficiently. The books deal with topical issues, such as *Parents and Schools* and organising and planning *Project Teaching*, and are written by authors with lots of practical advice and experiences to share.

Let's Investigate
Let's Investigate is an exciting range of photocopiable maths activity books giving open-ended investigative tasks. The series will complement and extend any existing maths programme. Designed to cover the 6 to 12-year-old age range these books are ideal for small group or individual work. Each book presents progressively more difficult concepts and many of the activities can be adapted for use throughout the primary school. Detailed teacher's notes outlining the objectives of each photocopiable sheet and suggesting follow-up activities have been included.